The Happiest Choice

Essential Tools for Everyone's Brain Feelings

Sage Liskey

Cultivating Happiness Checklist

Deal with any situation causing your depressed feelings. Constructively communicate anything that needs to be said. If that is not possible, or more time is needed:

- Schedule for the day and week ahead (Section 5.5).
- Eat a nutritious meal with anti-inflammatory foods (Section 7.1).
- Get outside to nature or someplace you haven't been for awhile (Section 9.2).
- Get enough sleep or take a break from work (Section 7.4).
- Avoid triggering foods and substances, especially inflammatory ones (Section 7.3).
- Take some time for yourself and enjoy one of your hobbies (Chapter 6).
- Go socialize or put yourself in a social environment (Section 6.14).
- No direct sun exposure? Take vitamin D daily (Section 7.2).
- Seek out a calming environment (Section 9.2).
- See a therapist (Section 9.5).
- Breathe deeply, meditate, and live in the present moment without thoughts of judgment (Section 6.1).

If You Have a Depressive Episode

Read the list of triggers in Chapter 4 to help figure out what the trigger was. Focus on addressing that trigger if possible and constructively communicating with any necessary parties. Here are some other options depending on how you feel:

- Remove yourself from overstimulating environments.
- Create a safe environment by cleaning your room, putting on music, etc.
- Seek out help from someone such as a friend, therapist, or doctor. Everything is easier with reassurance and support from others.
- Write. Process the thoughts in your head, recall the best moments of your life, or figure out where you want to be and how to get there.
- Meditate and practice mindfulness. Don't allow repetitive negative thoughts to take over. Find contentment and goodness in the present moment.
- Trust that the negative thoughts your brain creates are untrue and disconnected from your rationality. Trust that feelings of anxiety, paranoia, distrust, and disconnection will pass if you take care of yourself.
- Go to sleep.
- Play a game, read a book, or watch something that will occupy your mental energy.
- Admit yourself into a psychiatric ward and put yourself into the full care of medical professionals until you get better.
- Call a support line like the National Suicide Hotline at 1-800-273-8255.

Positivity Exercises

- Create an 'abundance mentality' by thinking about positive things as well as the possibilities of positive things in your life. Write a list of good things that happened today, this week, or month (Section 9.8).
- Express gratitude toward someone you appreciate, or volunteer for a cause (Section 6.2).
- Repeat one or two positive mantras for 5-20 minutes, one for an in breath, and one for an out breath (Section 6.1).
- Pray for, or mentally forgive people who have wronged you. (Section 6.1).
- Resolve conflicts, preferably with nonviolent communication (Section 10.4).
- Smile and laugh (Section 6.9).
- Breathe deeply and live in the present moment (Section 6.1).
- Accept what you fear the most and sprout happiness there (Section 9.11).

Printed in the United States of America
1st Edition

Edited by:
Sam Bennington, Jared Swanson, Julia Whisenant, Emma Banks, B.S., Alisha Kinlaw, Mitra Sticklen (activism chapter), Emily N Myers (activism chapter), Sonny Fisher, Larisa Varela, Elaine Russel, India Chilton, and Edmond Stansberry

Illustrated by:
Kerrida Hall: Molecules in Section 7.2 and 7.3.
Janine Hesse: All other illustrations.

Front Cover Illustration:
Janine Hesse, Sage Liskey

Cover Design:
Moth, Sage Liskey

Inside Design:
Sage Liskey

E-mail correspondence may be sent to:
sage.liskey@gmail.com

www.sageliskey.com
facebook.com/author.sage.liskey

ISBN-13: 978-0-9862461-0-4
ISBN-10: 0-9862461-0-7

Contents

- Nonviolent Communication: A Language of
  Compassion
- Pronoia Is The Antidote for Paranoia
- The Heart of the Buddha's Teaching
- That Which You Are Seeking Is Causing You to
  Seek
- Quiet
- Communicating Across the Divides in Our
  Everyday Lives

About This Book

I was inspired to write this guide when I saw a lack of inclusive manuals on coping with depression. I wanted to create something readable by all types of people without losing the reader in technical banter or long narratives. I wanted to keep it simple, but include information pertinent to anyone from soccer moms, activists, and stay-at-home-dads, to people of color, teenage punk rockers, and spiritualists. The collected information comes from nearly three years of research on depression and a lifetime of personal experiences with the symptoms. It is impossible to cover all aspects of depression, but I hope that herein you will find what matters most to individuals, families, friends, partners, and communities trying to work through it. That said, this is an introductory guide, and further research should be done regarding the topics discussed.

The creation of *The Happiest Choice* has been an amazing community effort. Many friends, coworkers, teachers, acquaintances, and even strangers have helped edit, illustrate, and provide ideas for this book. I am eternally grateful for their support and could not have made it this far without their kindness. I want to give special thanks to the University of Oregon R.O.A.R. Center, The University of Oregon Student Insurgent magazine, The Campbell Club Student Cooperative, and the many encouraging comments that people gave with each new booklet edition. Thank you!

Medical Statement

While I strongly believe in the methods outlined in this guide, **I am not a medical professional and none of this is meant to be medical advice.** Furthermore, even though primarily peer-reviewed research was used to collect information, new discoveries are made every day within the scientific community. **I therefore do not guarantee the accuracy of the information contained herein and expressly disclaim liability for errors and omissions in the contents of this book.** Ask a doctor, herbalist, nutritionist, or other health professional before trying these methods, or else use them at your own risk. **Again, this guide is not meant to be used to diagnose or treat depression or any other condition.** If you are having thoughts of harming yourself or others please call the National Suicide Hotline at 1-800-273-8255. They can offer confidential guidance, support, and help connect you with local resources.

1

How to Use
This Guide

This book will show you the abundance of options available and roads others have taken for cultivating happiness and coping with depression and depressed feelings. The information provided can be used in many ways, but the following will help you get the most use out of it:

- This book is most helpful if utilized as a preparatory tool. The outlined information can help you learn options of preparing mentally, physically, and materially for when a depressive episode or negative feelings come up. There is also information for those actively having a depressive episode.
- Read everything from the front to back cover; even section titles that seem uninteresting to you may actually hold very important content.
- While reading, write down or bookmark pages with techniques that you'd like to try or information that seems pertinent to

your lived experience. Don't overwhelm yourself though, there is a lot.

- Knowing your options, seek assistance from health professionals for learning more about the techniques discussed and for help applying them to your life.

- After an initial reading of the guide, the back cover, beginning pages, and table of contents may be used as quick reminders for the contents herein.

- A periodic re-reading from start to finish will be helpful as you discover more about your mental health and personal needs.

- The included resources (Chapter 14) and bibliography (Chapter 16) may be used for further reading.

2
You Have Options

The feelings of sadness, fear, and stress are an essential part of the human experience. They provide great learning opportunities by forcing a person to slow down and think about the world from another perspective. On the other hand, when gone unchecked, these feelings may become self-perpetuating and form into a physical and mental condition known as depression. While it is natural to experience depression, and in many lives impossible to avoid, it is possible to strengthen our resilience to it and find contentment when we have the right tools to do so. This process of coping with depression and depressed feelings is not about striving for constant happiness; it is about learning to healthfully balance thoughts and feelings in order to live a fulfilling life.

Anyone can become depressed when the right factors are in place. As a result, mild to severe depression affects millions of people worldwide *(Biomed)*. In the United States, most cases of depression are treated with pharmaceutical medicines. Pharmaceuticals work best for some people, but there are important things to know about them that many doctors fail to mention. First, the majority of people prescribed pharmaceutical antidepressants only feel better from a placebo effect *(Villarreal)*. These medicines are only effective for persons with severe depression, and have little to no impact on persons who experience mild depression *(Fournier; Kirsch I)*. Furthermore, even though they do work for some people, scientists are still unsure as to why *(Krishnan)*. They are often portrayed as simply fixing serotonin[A] levels, but a high or low level of serotonin has not actually been directly related to depression *(Hirschfeld)*. Secondly, when these medicines do work with people experiencing a genetic abnormality or chemical imbalance, they are much more effective when paired with methods that treat other root causes of depression such as malnutrition, inactivity, a stressful environment, communication styles, thinking patterns, or a traumatic past.

The following chapters are intended as an introduction to help you to identify depression, learn options for controlling it in yourself, and provide support to others. Most of the methods outlined will work with medications, but **be sure to see a medical professional before mixing any sort of herbal or off-the-shelf medicine with a prescribed medicine, or before going off of your medications.** There is no single cure-all that works for everyone, but depending on your personal needs, many options exist for cultivating happiness and contentment. It is your task to figure out which of these options work best for you. Good luck!

A   A neurotransmitter connected to happy feelings.

3
What Is Depression?

According to the U.S. National Library of Medicine, signs of depression include the following symptoms:

- Feeling sad or "empty."
- Feeling hopeless, irritable, anxious, or guilty.

- Loss of interest in favorite activities.
- Feeling very tired.
- Not being able to concentrate or remember details.
- Not being able to sleep, or sleeping too much.
- Overeating, or not wanting to eat at all.
- Thoughts of suicide, suicide attempts.
- Aches or pains, headaches, cramps, or digestive problems.

(MedlinePlus)

Clinically speaking depression is having several of these symptoms for extended periods of time. People are diagnosed with major depression if they have five or more of these symptoms last over two weeks, and minor depression if two to four of these symptoms are present for over two weeks. Dysthymia is like minor depression but is even milder and lasts at least two years *(Dysthymia)*. Note that depression can also be accompanied by other conditions with somewhat similar symptoms such as mania, schizophrenia, and bipolar disorder. These are not covered in this book, though several of the tools introduced may be equally helpful for dealing with them.

There are many sub-categories of depression. Even then, simply saying that someone has depression is misleading, because everyone experiences it uniquely. Everyone has different levels of the symptoms listed above and those symptoms are caused by different sources. When this guide refers to treating depression, it refers to treating the individual symptoms of depression specific to a person. To be clear about our use of terms, depression is another way of saying "extended suffering," and depressed feelings are the symptoms of depression listed above, but not necessarily the condition of depression itself.

4

What Causes Depression?

The physical and mental changes that depression creates can seemingly slip into one's life without much reason. In an attempt to explain the new mood, a person might blame it on how their life is going, or something unrelated that happened days or weeks prior. However, as you'll see, there are generally more direct reasons that explain why a person experiences depression or depressed feelings. Depression is caused by a combination of **potentials** and **triggers**. Things that increase the overall potential of experiencing depression and depressed feelings include:

- Depression running in the family and genetics (Section 7.2, 11.3) *(Levinson)*.
- Hormones (Section 11.1).
- Exposure to substances that cause genetic, hormonal, chemical, or neurological abnormalities (Section 7.3).
- Malnourishment (Section 7.1, 7.2).
- The time of year one is born (Section 11.3).

- Not being properly nourished while in the womb or not being breastfed as a child (Section 11.2, 11.3) *(Ryrie 23)*.
- Growing up in a negative space or experiencing traumatic events (Section 9.2, 9.17, 11.8).
- Growing up poor (Section 11.3) *(Kim)*.
- Cultural upbringing (Section 11.7).
- Discrimination (Section 11.8).
- Unmet social needs (Section 6.14).
- Communication styles (Chapter 10).
- Thinking patterns such as obsessing over a negative thought or judging people around you (Section 6.1, Chapter 9).
- Unmet needs (Section 9.1).
- Consuming foods or medications that cause inflammation in the body (Section 7.3) (*Kresser*).
- Things like low levels of serotonin, dopamine, and norepi-nephrine[A] do not cause depression as is often cited, but only increase the potential of experiencing depression *(Hirschfeld)*.

This list can be generalized into four broad categories: chronic genetic and chemical abnormalities, hormonal fluctuations, life events, and lifestyle choices. It may be difficult to discern which category or categories you fit into initially, but doing so will greatly help you find treatments for your depression (see Section 5.2).

"Triggers" put a person into the state of depression. They can include just about anything depending on the person, though some triggers are more common than others. These include things such as:

- Stressful or uncomfortable events like an argument or over-stimulating environment (Section 9.2)

A   Neurotransmitters connected to joyful and happy feelings.

- Not sleeping enough (Section 7.4).
- Thinking patterns such as obsessing over a negative thought or judging people around you (Section 6.1, 9.16).
- Eating too much or not enough (Chapter 7, Section 7.1).
- Sensitivity to certain foods (Section 7.1).
- The intake of alcohol and other substances (Section 7.3).
- Viewing and/or listening to certain media, especially news stories and movies, books, music, etc. depicting violence, anger, and sadness (Section 9.6).
- Viewing and/or listening to media for an extended period of time (Section 9.6).
- Not enough social interaction (Section 6.14).
- Staying inside (Section 6.3, 7.2, 9.2).
- Withdrawal symptoms from addictions to things such as food, media, drugs, medicines, and alcohol (Section 7.3, 8.1).
- Inability to cope with societal pressures such as appearance, fitting in, gender expectations, and other cultural norms (Section 6.14, 9.7, 9.13, 9.18, 11.7, 11.8).
- A "potential" can act as a "trigger" with factors like sleeplessness and malnourishment.

5
The Road Map of Coping

1. Desiring change and a feeling of contentment.
2. Becoming aware of your "potentials" and "triggers."
3. Creating an action plan for addressing sources of suffering.
4. Creating a self-care schedule that incorporates the action plan.
5. Reforming habits and other sources of suffering.

The goal with this road map is to create long-standing contentment and stability, rather than short-term happiness. Note that this will take time and a certain amount of trial and error. As personal discoveries are made you will have the choice of altering your lifestyle and ways of thinking. It might be frightening and difficult at times, but will pay off in the end by a renewed sense of peace and purpose. A depressive episode can completely change your personality and perception of the world, and so when depression does strike, it is important to be prepared with as many tools as possible for finding your way back to a state of contentment. The contents of this chapter will reveal the primary tools you can use to apply coping mechanisms to your life. There are other tools throughout this guide, but the tools in this chapter build a foundation to work from.

5.1 - Desiring Change and a More Content Life

A basic starting point to coping with depression is acknowledging that you are experiencing depression and it is impacting your ability to enjoy life. Perhaps you already know this, but the connection is not always easy, especially with the myths and stigmas surrounding depression. It is also common to feel crummy but not acknowledge those feelings as signs of depression. In a lifetime, most everyone will experience depression. It is just a label that you can use to better understand yourself and how to reach a stronger sense of fulfillment.

Sometimes depression will go away on its own, but when wanting to shorten the length of time you are depressed, you need to desire that change to happen. This is not always easy as motivational energy is sapped away within a depressive episode. Developing a set of activities or a routine that convinces your mind into wanting change and breaks apathetic behaviors is useful. Here is a list of things that I have used to fight apathy:

- Don't rationalize feelings or create self-fulfilling prophecies. For instance, instead of thinking of whether or not you'll enjoy an activity with friends, just go do it. Don't tell yourself that you won't enjoy the activity, because you have no idea how you'll actually feel once there. If you really aren't in a good space to be around others you can always leave after you've given the activity a decent try.
- Put yourself around people by going to a cafe, park, mall, or other space. If you live with others, at the very least get out of your room and to your living room or front porch. Seeing

other peoples' interactions and emotions can be enlivening and you may even have a chance social encounter. Often what knocks me out of an apathetic state is either chatting with a good stranger or running into an old friend I haven't seen in awhile.

- Watch an emotionally stimulating movie. With movies you see people having fun, making friends, falling in love, competing, creating, winning, and generally doing amazing things that you could also be doing. I personally get jealous of these fictitious or romanticized lives and remind myself that I want all those things too. Because movies have a complete story experienced in a single sitting, they seem to work better than television shows, video games, or fiction books. These other forms of media more often make my mood worse. Try movies with characters and situations that you can relate to rather than things like unrealistic Hollywood action flicks.

- Compete with yourself or others in an activity. It's much harder to be apathetic when you have a goal and are trying to succeed.

- Maintain a schedule with obligations that must be fulfilled. Even if you are feeling crummy, being required to stay engaged with others and your hobbies will prevent apathy from sticking around for long; that is so long as you are taking measures of self-care as well.

When you desire change, insight to solutions may be found in many places, including those that were previously meaningless to you. Books, memories, and words from friends hold more meaning in a place of inner turmoil. Reforming habits is also easier. The desire for change within a depressive episode is not just a time we desperately want to learn and grow; it is an ideal time to find and apply creative solutions to our difficulties.

5.2 - Awareness of "Potentials" and "Triggers"

To become aware of your "potentials" and "triggers," review the list in Chapter 4. For "potentials," explore what your childhood was like, difficult life experiences, and your nutrient intake. Depression caused by genetic abnormalities is difficult to uncover, but may be a likely culprit if other treatment methods do not respond well or depression runs in your family. If you have never experienced depression until your 30s, 40s, or 50s, or if your depressive episodes occur cyclically on a daily or monthly basis, you may have hormonal depression. For more help, read the sections cited in Chapter 4.

As for "triggers," ask yourself what event or events triggered the depressive episode? How did it make you feel? How did the episode end or what alleviated your emotions? Form the "triggers" into a simple and accessible list of direct consequences. For example, "If I don't _____, I will feel/think/behave _____." Or, "If _____ happens, I will feel/think/behave _____." See the end of this book for a helpful "My Mind" sheet to fill out. Reading this list will help you acknowledge that there is a reason for the way you feel and that it is not the norm. In this manner, you can focus on dealing with the cause rather than the negative thoughts and feelings created from being depressed. It will also give you a road map of what you need to do in the future in order to either avoid the causes of your depression or transform those causes into something non-triggering.

As you discover the things that trigger depressed feelings and depression in your life, it is important to turn down or suggest alternatives to offers that involve these triggers. This may mean ending or not pursuing certain friendships. It may also mean having conversations about how you experience reality and have difficulty with certain movies, words, behaviors, actions, etc. You can say "I'd rather _____," "not today," "I want to leave," or "I dislike this, can you/we _____?" Some triggers are deeply ingrained and may require reforming habits too.

5.3 - Forming and Deforming Habits

With awareness of your "potentials" and "triggers" you can begin altering your lifestyle. This might include things like your environment, friends, and especially habits. Habits are both physical and mental. You can have a habit of brushing your teeth, or of panicking when you see someone. An extended period of depression may cause a mental habit of it and create anxiety or sadness more easily in the future. It is therefore important to deal with existing depressive triggers as soon as possible and prevent new triggers from forming.

According to Charles Duhigg, a habit has three parts to it, the "habit cues," the habit itself, and a reward for performing the habit *(Gross. Habits)*. An example would be the smell of cookies (the habit cue) leading you to purchase and eat a cookie (the habit) which in turn satisfies your sweet tooth (the reward). Habit cues include anything from sights and sounds to smells and feelings. Once the habit has initiated, the brain actually automates the task and is free to think about other thoughts and actions. Everyone forms habits at a different rate, though three weeks has become a popularized number for people to strive for when attempting to embed a new habit *(Layton)*. If you are performing a behavior regularly enough, it should stay permanently wired within your neural makeup after this amount of time *(Delude)*. This is great for healthy habits, but also makes breaking an unhealthy habit exceptionally difficult. Even if you do break a habit, being around old "habit cues" can quickly make the habit reform *(Gross. Habits)*. This is especially challenging as the rewards for an unhealthy behavior are often more immediate than the rewards for a healthy behavior. So how can you change your behaviors?

Tips for Forming Habits

- Repeat the behavior often, at regular intervals *(Layton)*.
- Start small. Form one habit at a time, and perform that habit a few times a week rather than every day *(Layton)*.
- Schedule the habit with specifics of when and for how long. For instance, for 30 minutes on Mondays, Wednesdays, and Fridays at 9:00AM I will _____ *(Layton)*. If your work or life schedule shifts around, make a time reference to accommodate it, such as "when I get off work" or "after I eat dinner."
- Make the reward for the habit visible. Keep a daily log of how you feel from performing the habit, or treat yourself to something nice (but healthy!) for accomplishing the behavior.
- Make a game out of the activity, either competing against yourself or other people.
- Work on forming the habit with someone else, such as an exercise buddy. This way you will both feel obligated to not skip your exercise schedule. You can also seek help through counselors, therapists, and support groups.
- If you are not motivated to do a healthy activity, try thinking of it in a more interesting way. For instance, "to love my whole body," "to document magic," "to get away from those silly humans," "to get artistic inspiration," or, "to see my tree friends."
- Make good habits more visible. For instance, put supplements next to your bed, healthy foods on the kitchen counter, or a book you should read in your bag.
- Force yourself to do it. It may be uncomfortable, but really, you're never going to want to do something you don't feel motivated to do, or have yet to create a habit for. As Amy Cuddy says, "fake it till you make it" *(Cuddy)*.

Tips for Deforming Habits

- Recognize the "habit cues" and rewards for a given habit *(Gross. Habits)*.
- If a "habit cue" such as stress or seeing junk food causes you to perform an unhealthy habit, train yourself to perform a healthy habit when you receive those habit cues instead *(Layton)*.
- Remove unhealthy "habit cues" from your life if possible, even if it means ending a friendship or changing your living space.
- Break "habit cues" by changing your environment. The easiest way to change a habit is by doing so on vacation, because you are removed from the "habit cues" of your normal environment *(Gross. Habits)*.
- Put the habit just a little further out of reach so you think twice before initiating it. For instance, temporarily block websites with a blocking program, or place an addicting food out of sight.

To learn more about habits, read *The Power of Habit* by Charles Duhigg, or B.F. Skinner's research work on "operant conditioning." There are also smart phone and computer applications available for helping you form and deform habits. One free habit building application called Habit RPG <www.habitrpg.com> even incorporates addictive aspects of video games. You start by creating an avatar and then earn experience and gold for completing your set tasks. In turn you level up and can purchase personally set rewards for yourself and gear for your avatar.

5.4 - Action Plan

An action plan lays out how to deal with your potentials and triggers. It covers things like habits, people, and environments that you could add or remove from your life to find a stronger sense of contentment and happiness. The plan might start with identifying the biggest thing you want to change, how you could live that new life with or without it, monetary needs, different class times for learning something, obstacles to overcome, and in general all the steps required to get from point A to point B. Schedule in the time you need to do these individual tasks, and get to it. The following bubble diagram is one method of creating an action plan.

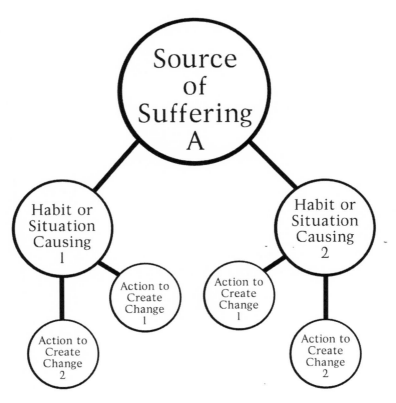

5.5 - Time for Self-Care and Scheduling

Even if you always seem busy, you can still find the time to take care of yourself. If you can't read a book, listen to an audio-book. If you can't go to the gym, exercise while sitting down, or stretch while brushing your teeth. If you can't join a meditation group, meditate while eating food, or before going to sleep. In other words, combine self-care with the things you already do on a daily basis. You might also remove certain things or at least decrease the use of them in your life, such as using the internet and watching television. It all comes down to reforming how you think things should be done. Creating a schedule will also help you find that precious time.

A schedule acts as a reminder for what you need to and want to do, and helps you find more time to enjoy life and practice self-care. With depression the desire to do anything often plummets. Plans get canceled and work productivity slows. Not only that, but daily routines may become unenjoyable. A schedule is a very effective navigation tool for not losing your course, and can take many forms. It can be a single piece of paper, a day-to-day planner book, a calendar, a phone application with automated reminders, or all four. I prefer a weekly planner, but you do have to remember to check it every day. Make sure to cover activities for your personal health first, and then include time for other things like volunteering, media entertainment, and hosting events. Scheduling too much time for others, or too much in general, might create stress and hardship and make you forget to do things like exercise, sleep, and eat healthfully. Once you've completed a task, it's especially nice to cross it off as an accomplishment. Depending on how you personally experience depression, you may want to schedule your entire day out, including waking up, eating, and so on.

Another scheduling technique is creating a list of activities to do if you feel a certain way or something triggering happens. The Icarus Project (see Section 14.2) calls this a "mad map." To create a mad map, write your "escalators," or negative emotions, and next to that your "de-escalators," or actions that make you feel better when sad, anxious, and so on. Below that, list people to call at any time to talk with. This should be put somewhere easily accessible so that you will read it when needed. You could also include a list of specific things that cause you stress and how you coped effectively with them in the past. See the end of this guide for a slightly modified example called "My Mind."

Knowledge of your potentials and triggers and how to form and deform habits, as well as creating an action plan and schedule are the basic tools for applying self-care to your life. The remainder of this guide documents various triggers as well as things that can help lower one's potential for experiencing depression and anxiety. Note that not all these techniques will work for everyone. Sometimes there is culture in the way, sometimes there is money in the way, sometimes there are personal interests in the way, and that's okay–there are many options to choose from. What makes one person happy and content might do nothing for another, or even trigger depression or depressed feelings in them, so it is your job to experiment. What activities, foods, medicines, environments, thoughts, and nutrients make you feel better? Which don't? Apply this knowledge to discovering the life you want to live.

6
Activities and Hobbies

Not only do things like running, art, writing, traveling, music, collecting, potlucks, and puzzles bring fulfillment and potentially connect you with new friends, activities and hobbies like these also help keep the brain from obsessing over negative thoughts. This is especially true when experiencing something wholly new or getting your adrenaline pumping. Try out activities from the newspaper, classes, or online from websites like <www.craigslist.com> or <meetup.com>. Activities that help others are especially fulfilling by occupying your time with making a difference and boosting self-esteem and self-worth. Find what nourishes your well-being. Schedule all activities into a planner or to-do list, or set up dates with friends so you feel more inclined to do the task. The following section documents some of the best activities and hobbies for coping with depression.

6.1 - Deep Breathing, Meditation, Mindfulness, Prayer, and Rituals

Deep Breathing

Slow and deep breathing (breathing into the abdomen or diaphragm) can provide a quick reduction in blood pressure and anxiety *(Cuda)*. According to physician Esther Sternberg, this intentional action prevents the production of stress hormones and in turn allows the body to calm itself. Reforming shallow breathing into a habit of deep breathing could even provide a long-term method of stress reduction. If you are unfamiliar with deep breathing, slowly take a deep breath in through your nose. Your belly should expand before you exhale through either your nose or mouth.

Meditation

Regular meditation improves mood and prevents depression *(Paula)*. There are many forms of meditation including mindfulness (Vipassana), zazen, transcendental, kundalini, qi gong, guided visualization, trance-based, and heart rhythm meditation

(Bair). The primary goal of most of these practices is to gain better control over the mind and body, but different styles accomplish different things in different ways.

Mindfulness

One of the most popular forms of meditation is mindfulness meditation. Why can words, sounds, gestures, images, and other stimuli cause sadness, anger, and anxiety? It is because the mind fuels them with thoughts and judgments and in turn obsesses over the stimuli in a negative way. With mindfulness you learn that there is an option to think or not to think, and that it is okay and often healthy not to. This is because the more you focus on something the more intense it becomes. Obsessing over negative or positive things (such as a person you really like) can cause suffering, so when one trained in mindfulness becomes aware of those thought streams, they move their focus to the sensations of the present moment *(Grohol)*.

Researchers have found that the act of regularly focusing on the present moment gradually "[increases] activity on the left side of the prefrontal cortex, which is associated with joyful and serene emotions" *(Meditation)*. The practice has been shown to decrease anxiety, increase brain gray matter[A], and prevent age related memory loss *(Lazar)*. Another benefit of practicing mindfulness is that it enhances our sensations. By removing judgments, getting out of our thoughts, and focusing wholly on what is, sights become more beautiful, smells are more aromatic, feelings are more sensual, food is more tasteful, and music sounds more pleasant. It is a sort of joyful perspective that, with practice, can be maintained indefinitely and transforms the whole world into a new oasis to experience.

Mindfulness is not an act of avoidance, but rather an aware-

A Brain gray matter controls some muscles, senses, and memory functions (Miller).

ness of what is healthy and what causes suffering while fully experiencing life. Some practice "living in the present moment" as ignoring the future and not making plans, but this is unhealthy and often harmful to others. A healthy practice of "living in the present moment" is being aware of your actions and where your thoughts are, whether in the past, present, or future, and how those thoughts and actions impact yourself and the world around you. Mindfulness can be used all the time, or simply when you notice a need to step back from your thoughts for a while. It might be likened to your focus on a really good movie, or a rush of adrenaline from playing sports or competing in a game. It is total focus and immersion into what is happening right now.

Mindfulness is a skill that takes time to develop, but there are many ways of practicing it anywhere and anytime. These include things like maintaining awareness of the sensations of your body, of an action you are performing, of a conversation, or of thoughts that arise, but the most common way of practicing mindfulness is following your breath. Your breath is always with you, and so it is a reliable focal point. The more you practice being aware of your breath, the easier being aware of other sensations and aspects of your life will be. Closing your eyes will help prevent distractions, but you can certainly do this practice with your eyes open. Follow the air moving under your nostrils and down into your belly, and then follow it back out. Keeping count of your breaths or saying "in" with each inward breath and "out" with each outward breath may help maintain your focus. Try doing this breathing awareness exercise for five to ten minutes daily as you first begin, and challenge yourself to increase it to 20 or 30 minutes a day as you get better. Thoughts and judgments of the past, present, and future may arise, but let them flow past and return your focus to the sensations of the present moment found in your breathing. Sometimes I note the emotions attached to a thought before returning to my breath by saying something like "I'm really excited about that," or "I have some anger built up around this person," just to acknowledge it and not ignore what I'm feeling in that present moment.

While focusing wholly on your breathing or other sensations, you cannot be distracted by sadness or anxiety. At a basic level mindfulness provides us with a calming period where we can step back from extreme emotions prior to dealing with a situation in constructive rationality. You might use mindfulness when, for example, your boss critiques your work because it does not meet their standards. Instead of making yourself feel bad by obsessing over the critique with thoughts of worry and anxiety, focus on your breathing, a vase, the sunlight, a conversation, or any emotionally neutral stimuli. Do not follow negative thoughts into the past or the future. Take up the space used for making yourself feel bad with the small details of your surroundings and your body's sensations. While I believe not labeling anything helps you focus on sensations better, it may be useful to silently state different details of an environment when first learning visual mindfulness such as "I am sitting in a wooden chair," "there is a white glass lamp on the table," and "I am turning a brass door handle." This task is even easier to do in movement. While walking, stay present by focusing on an object until you pass it, and then change your focus to a new object. Look deeply into the details, noting small textures and colors. Another option is to sit with an emotion and focus on it, fully experiencing the sensations it creates. Doing so will make the emotion go away much quicker because your thoughts are not fueling it with constant reminders. Once you have calmed down, use other techniques, such as writing, to process and deal with the situation. One more idea is to train yourself to hear natural mindfulness bells. These stimuli remind you to focus on your breath and can include things like cars honking, a cell phone buzzing, or an angry person talking. Natural mindfulness bells are great because they rewrite how your brain processes an event by creating a new and positive habit for habit cues you normally find stressful or triggering *(Layton)*. With enough practice it is possible to find calmness where once there was turmoil, just by breathing.

Resources to learn mindfulness can be found at <http://www.mindful.org/mindfulness-practice>, in the writings of Thich Nhat Hanh, and the book *How To Train A Wild Elephant & Other Adventures in Mindfulness*. More helpful, however, is joining a meditation group or taking a class. Yoga and tai-chi are options that integrate stretching, movement, and meditation together. Another option is joining a sangha, or community, that practices under the non-dogmatic teachings of Thich Nhat Hanh and offers mindfulness meditation for free or by donation. They practice a mixture of walking, sitting, guided, listening, speaking, and eating meditation. For help finding a sangha near you, or starting a sangha, go to <www.thichnhathanhfoundation.org>. There is also Wake Up <wkup.org> for young-adult and youth-based sanghas. Yet another option is Vippasana Meditation. Vippasana is a mindfulness meditation where beginners are generally required to complete a free 10 day silent retreat before moving on in the discipline <www.dhamma.org>. Whichever course you take, attending a retreat is very beneficial for creating a space where you fully focus on forming a habit of meditation. There are also online podcasts, smart phone applications, and communities of people encouraging each other to find mindful awareness.

Prayer

To stay in the present, it is also useful to make peace with the past. Prayer, especially "prayers releasing hurts" and "prayers of blessings" on persons who have offended you can help improve mood *(Boelens)*. This means taking time to forgive yourself for things you might blame or judge yourself for, and wishing well on and forgiving people who have hurt you in the past. While often associated with a religious or spiritual lifestyle, prayer can also be practiced by a person with a secular worldview. This 'prayer' might even take the form of a mantra meditation, where a positive or insightful phrase is said with each inward and outward breath. Take some time right now to focus on moving onward and transforming negative memories into memories of growth and healing.

Rituals

The act of holding a ritual creates a space to deepen your emotions, commitments, or your desire to change. The components of the ritual are generally symbolic, but necessary to strengthen your feelings surrounding your goal. You have to believe in that goal to actualize it. In this space that you hold for yourself or with others, you might remind yourself what is important to you, move on from hurtful memories, end emotional ties to a friendship or relationship, or accept your transition into a new life. Some common rituals include church, new and full moon ceremonies, and holidays.

A ritual of letting go of the old might involve writing out all the frustrations you have on paper, and then with a strong desire to let go of what is written, burn the grievances. Another idea is to collect relics of a difficult time and bury them underground; soil organisms can take care of the memories from there.

You could also answer questions about what motivates you or what keeps you happy. To prevent dependency it is suggested not basing this on any one person or thing, but rather on what keeps you happy on your own. Some examples are waking up to watch the sunset each morning or lighting a candle for someone you respect before going to bed.

6.2 - Gratitude and Volunteering

Expressing gratitude toward others alleviates depression and improves happiness *(Seligman)*. Gratitude for others can be expressed through acts such as gifts, letters, donations, or even just a few kind words of appreciation for someone's existence. Gratitude is especially powerful when done at random without reasons such as a birthday or anniversary. You can also show gratitude by volunteering with different groups. Partaking in volunteer opportunities builds job skills, introduces you to new people, and provides a sense of fulfillment. Search online or look at your local newspaper and see what's available in your area. If you do volunteer though, watch out for negativity and groups that try to destroy rather than create something. Read more in *Advocacy, Volunteering, and Activism* (Chapter 12).

6.3 - Gardening, Farming, and Soil Bacteria

By gardening, you not only feel fulfilled through meeting the essential human need for food and nurturing other lifeforms, you also get sunlight (vitamin D), exercise, fresh air, and exposure to a bacteria called Mycobacterium vaccae. Research conducted by Dr.

Christopher Lowry indicates that Mycobacterium vaccae is an antidepressant and prevents inflammatory disorders like asthma *(Marano 57)*. Much more research is being done into M. Vaccae that suggests it has other health benefits as well. Accordingly, Dr. Lowry has proposed the "hygiene hypothesis," which states that many people today are sick because they are too clean and not getting outside enough. This makes sense, because our bodies rely on a symbiotic relationship with bacteria to function. In fact, for every human cell in our body, there are 10 microbial cells *(Gross. Bacterial)*. If we lack bacteria that our bodies have traditionally used to work, then the natural consequence is that our bodies cannot function to their full capacity. Some of my friends even stopped needing to take their pharmaceutical anti-depressants when they began working on an organic farm. This could have been caused by a number of factors, but it was still intriguing to hear. Farming has the added benefit of usually being removed from city stresses such as pollutants, cars, loud sounds, overwhelming stimuli, and, depending on where you live, ugly city aesthetics.

6.4 - Writing

Writing has been an effective tool for me when coping with depression. Putting words on paper or a computer helps me process thoughts and stressful situations as well as record my life. It is nice to be able to look back and know my mental and physical accomplishments, or pick up on unhealthy situations and habits. Writing a thought or feeling also makes it stable and concrete, so that it does not have to be continuously repeated as it would be in my head. In this way a thought can be developed rather than dwelled upon.

Part of fighting depression is in recognizing that you are depressed and how that influences your thoughts and feelings. The world experienced from a depressed state appears starkly different.

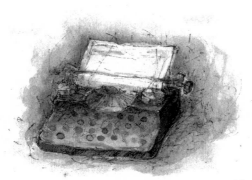

In this altered state, you may lash out at yourself or others, and often in ways that hurt the "un-depressed you." By processing your thoughts and feelings, you will better understand their basis in reality and how to deal with them accordingly. Realize that your friends have no reason to dislike you, or that strangers are not judging you poorly. Also consider:

- Write a list of positive affirmations that you feel are true for yourself and put it on your wall to read each morning when you wake up. Include things like, "I am strong," "I love myself," and, "the world has many opportunities for me."

- Pose questions to yourself or find thought provoking materials (such as horoscopes, books, or movies) that create questions to explore your personality. Challenge your moral fiber!

- Write about happy memories from your past, or about who, what, and where you want to be in the future. Recalling the happiest moments of your life can be very uplifting and give you a sense of something that you want to strive for in the future. Keeping photo albums and printing digital photographs may help in this process! Photos on the computer have their place but lack a certain quality, depth, and importance to them. Writing about your ideal future will give you ideas about things to change in the present.

- Write about yourself from a third person perspective as if a good friend were talking about you. For some, this activity will be helpful in separating thoughts one has about themselves from the reality of who they are in the world.

- To highlight the positive aspects of your personal life, try taking some time each day to write what you were grateful for, made you happy, or went well. Even doing a single overview writing for the week or month is a great exercise to focus on what is good in life.

- Sometimes a situation that causes you grief is tied to a common trait that has led to similar situations in the past, and that common trait is sometimes tied to other traits that assist in that grief. It can therefore be helpful to unravel these situations in writing and see where they lead. When I think I might be onto something, I write, "there is something deeper here" and analyze how my feelings, fears, past occurrences, needs, desires, actions, habits, thinking patterns, culture, etc. all play a role in what is causing me discomfort.

- Create a bubble diagram to organize thoughts and sources of suffering (see Section 5.4 for an example of a bubble diagram).

6.5 - Reading

Reading materials provide a lot of insight about your life and the interactions with the people around you. Reading news, magazines, online articles, horoscopes, scriptures, and fiction and non-fiction books also provide talking points when socializing. Chapter 14 includes a list of resources with books and websites that have provided life-changing information to me. Studying psychology can also help illuminate why your brain works the way it does.

6.6 - Make and Experience Arts and Crafts

Art is a means of expressing what cannot be said with plain words. Over human existence it has been a useful tool for personal discovery and relating stories to the masses. Making art, or participating in art therapy sessions can actually reduce depression, anxiety, and hopelessness *(Judith; Hughs)*. With art you actively use your mind and body to stay present and also are able to self-analyze in a sort of meditative way. You might also feel a self-esteem boost from having a physical relic of something you have accomplished, or by receiving positive feedback for your completed artwork (if you are willing to share it). You don't just have to make stereotypical pieces of art like paintings either. Why not play music, make informational booklets from your old essays, publish a community map of your favorite stores, crochet a rug, create a website, reupholster your couch, or build a strange table out of recycled objects? The sky's the limit, unless you build a space shuttle! When you make something yourself, even painting the trim on your house, you create a deeper connection and understanding with it in a way that is enlivening to see.

Experiencing art may have a similar effect. While listening to a concert, walking through an art museum, or just browsing internet websites such as <www.deviantart.com> there is a chance that you run into something so beautiful and real that it wakes you from a sort of slumber. Art deepens our understanding of the world we live in by highlighting various aspects of it in an entertaining way. Artwork also connects us with others who have had similar experiences to our own, shattering the concept that we are alone in our struggles. The experience of artwork is generally heightened by seeing it in person. Unlike on a computer, the art's original may be massive, full of texture, contain distinctive sounds, or be part of an interactive exhibit. Just watch out for consuming too much art and disconnecting from reality. For more information see *Media Addiction and Staying in Tune with "Reality"* (Section 9.6).

6.7 - Listen to Music and Background Noise

So long as you enjoy it, any type of music can improve mood *(Kemper)*. Contrary to what some think, music stereotypically viewed as angry, such as death metal, is likely listened to as a symptom of depression rather than being the cause of a person's negative feelings *(Scheel)*. That said, I have experienced intensified anger, sadness, and depression brought on by listening to sad or angry music. In fact, many studies have shown that using aggressive outlets to release angry feelings actually increases the incidence of future aggressive acts *(Russell)*. It might be better to react to difficult situations by playing a calming or thought-provoking playlist instead. Be mindful of how music impacts you, and make sure it does not become a means of completely avoiding emotions or processing thoughts. For more information see *Media Addiction and Staying in Tune with "Reality"* (Section 9.6)

Another option for your ears is natural sound. If you want to create a calming environment, or if noises from things like doors, voices, and trains stress you out or keep you awake, listen to soothing recorded background sounds like rain, wind, and ocean waves. Download any number of nature's noises online and put them on loop to play indefinitely, or just turn on a fan. There are also smart phone applications available with large sets of calming sounds to choose from.

6.8 - Go on Adventures

Take a break from your day to day life and go on an adventure. This might be a celebration, an educational retreat, camping, hiking, or visiting another country. Doing so lets you clear your head, meet new people, collect stories to tell, and discover new insights. The adrenaline rush that new experiences create also gives the body and mind a nice feeling. It is especially fun to connect with others who share your niche interests such as at car shows or comic book fests. For me, adventures are more meaningful if they take some effort to organize. A spontaneous adventure can still be fun and life-changing, but the anticipation leading up to a planned event is really great. To connect with hobbyist groups look online and in the newspaper for conventions and meetings in your area. For more information see *Maintain A Positive Environment* (Section 9.2).

6.9 - Smile and Laugh

Our bodies associate smiling with expressing positive feelings and happiness *(Lienhard)*. Even if you aren't feeling happy, try giving a genuine smile and you might at least have a small break from negative emotions. Also try putting yourself in a social situation where other people are around because smiling is actually a social cue *(Ruiz-Belda)*. My experience is that I express positive emotions more strongly when others are expressing them with me, so movies, memes, music, etc. are often better in groups.

When life is especially stressful, it's also nice to laugh. Although sometimes difficult, a stand-up comedy, funny book, quirky movie, or giggly friend can provide a certain entertainment that connects you to the idea that life has a happy side. Happiness is a skill, and just like any skill, takes practice if you are not naturally talented at it.

6.10 - Massage Therapy

Massage therapy has a number of therapeutic benefits including "reducing pain, increasing alertness, diminishing depression, and enhancing immune function" *(Field, Tiffany M)*. However, the massage must be given with at least moderate pressure for these benefits to take place *(Field T)*. Light pressure will not work, so specify this to your massage therapist or buddy and get relaxed.

6.11 - Acupuncture

Acupuncture may be effective at temporarily relieving symptoms of depression and anxiety, but research results vary with general acupuncture techniques *(Zhang-Jin; Smith, Caroline)*. Those studies aside, it has induced a calming state when I've used it, and acupuncture studies using the NADA (National Acupuncture Detoxification Association) protocol seem more promising. The NADA protocol uses points in the ear to help relieve a whole host of symptoms, including depression and anxiety, drug addiction, and PTSD *(Kenneth)*. Acupuncture can be expensive, but to reduce costs search for community acupuncture clinics that offer sliding scale fees and treat multiple people in the same room.

6.12 - Light Therapy

Light therapy uses high intensity lights to simulate sunlight and can prevent seasonal affective disorder (SAD). SAD is a type of depression generally experienced in places with limited sunlight during the wintertime. Some evidence indicates that light therapy can also help prevent non-seasonal depression, especially with persons who are indoors most of the day *(Young, "Bright")*. Treatment times vary, but generally for the full effects to take place a session in front of a 10,000 lux light will last 30 minutes, and a session in front of a 2500 lux light will last 2 hours *(Columbia)*. These lights can be purchased online.

6.13 - Calming Scents of Aromatherapy

Certain smells are very calming for the mind, so see what you like and keep a bit of it with you whenever you need a peaceful break. These might take the form of herbs, essential oils, incense sticks, or flowers. Some smells that my friends and I enjoy include lavender, basil, sage, sandalwood, palo santo, roses, bergamot, mint, ylang ylang, cinnamon, cloves, and soil.

6.14 - Friendships, Relationships, and Community

Friendship

While depression and social withdrawal often go hand-in-hand, try to challenge yourself to spend time with others. My experience is that even if I don't want to socialize, I feel better if I do. This may not be the case for everyone all the time, but humans are social creatures who thrive off of one another. Friends provide support for when you're feeling down, share happy moments, and motivate you to do activities. Making friends is an art that anyone can become good at, but it takes practice and time. Learn what works and what doesn't when communicating with a new person. Be sure you are consistent with social gatherings, or keep a ritual of contacting at least one person a day to make plans with or write a letter to. Have activities to do rather than just lounging around, or ask an acquaintance to teach you something they are passionate about. Also spend as much time socializing with people face-to-face as you can. While blogs, forums, games, chat rooms, etc. can lead to friendships, Facebook usage has been shown to increase depressed feelings after use *(Kross)*. It is healthier to only use social media such as Facebook for organizing and learning about events in real life rather than trying to maintain friendships on it. Face-to-face encounters also provide certainty for what people are saying. Using interactions through electronic devices as a reason to believe someone doesn't like you might not be the best idea, because so much has to be assumed by the various forms of communication which are lost (tone, non-verbal hand and facial gestures, etc.). For more information read *Communication* (Chapter 10).

If making friends is difficult, you might want to consider how you are expressing yourself or how you are relating to others. Try your best to assert needs for maintaining your mental health though, even if that sometimes means ending a friendship. This process is an opportunity for personal growth. Know that friendship is two-sided, and both sides must provide something that the other needs such as social contact, shared interests, food, and so forth. Both sides must also have the time to take on a new friend; though people can stay acquaintances for years and then develop a close friendship. No matter what your problems are or what interests you have, someone will likely share them. It's just a matter of figuring out who! This begins with putting yourself out into the social world and being willing to make mistakes. Embracing labels, such as poet, artist, gardener, entrepreneur, etc. can be useful for connecting with groups too. See Section 10.2 for a description of introverts and extroverts that may also be helpful for your social life.

While friends may be great at cheering you up while you are down, remember that suffering tends to create more suffering. Repetitively complaining or venting about the same thing is draining to others, and as mentioned in the chapter *Thoughts for Change*, is generally not a constructive outlet for getting better. If you have a lot of thoughts to process, seeking the aid of a therapist may be better than expending the energies of a friend. Unless your complaints are being used to work toward a healthy solution, consider transforming your social time used for venting into healthy outlets like exercising or cooking a nice meal. This is not to say that you should keep silent about your troubles, just be conscious that too much sharing of sadness, frustration, or anger, especially over the same thing, may be difficult for others. Also, just because you want to say something does not mean that it has to be said. Walk in another person's shoes and give yourself time to calm emotions and process thoughts rationally; doing so will make your friends love you all the more.

Pets such as cats and dogs also help with one's social life because they make fairly forgiving friends and are easy to get along with. That is, so long as you take care of them properly. They can also help one learn about compassionate behavior, an essential skill with human friends.

Friendship is essential, but be wary of basing all your happiness on one person or a group of people. Doing so will eventually lead to a lot of pain because you will not have anyone if those social ties end. Beyond maintaining a diverse network of friends, be your own best friend, take care of yourself and do things for you that make you happy. There is also the option of having an imaginary friend or two with non-living creatures such as a stuffed animal or piece of artwork. Having backups when friends bail or go sour is important to recouping faster, and to not being upset about the chaos and spontaneous decisions made by others.

Do you feel safe and comfortable around your friends? Can you be yourself? If a friendship is not working out or consuming your time from making more meaningful friendships, it is okay to step back or end that friendship. This might involve a formal conversation, seeking out new friends, removing or unfollowing that person on social media websites, or holding a ritual (Section 6.1) to help let go and move forward.

Relationships

Friendship can also develop romantically into a relationship. Relationships should ideally not be sought out as a coping mechanism for depression, but only as a point of mutual love. This is because codependent and abusive relationships are more likely and harder to remove yourself from when you are in a depressed state of mind. A healthy relationship involves communication, consent, and, maintaining other friendships. Through this you are given purpose and a person to feel safe around, but the emotions often come in extremes too. You will almost definitely experience extreme happiness and extreme sorrow at some point. Even with those extremes in mind, sharing love is worth a lot in life. Of course, you don't need to engage in a relationship to express or feel love; that can be done through friendships.

Be wary of spending all your time with a partner. Doing so will make the end of a relationship much harder. Continue to seek out new friends and spend time with old ones, even if a lover is also your "best" or "only true friend." If a partner is physically or verbally abusive, manipulative, does not respect boundaries, does not communicate well, or needs more than you can give, it may not be the right relationship for you. Even if breakups are hard, there are many other people to fall in love with, and being your own stable person is most important.

One useful technique for maintaining stability is to get into a relationship with yourself. Love yourself. Go out with yourself. Do things that make you feel fulfilled and good. Acknowledge when you aren't spending enough time with you, and make it known!

Community

If your current living situation is isolating, consider joining a community. Community living and renting a house with others is great in that it takes a lot of pressure off of meeting people, makes finding social events easier, lowers individual expenses, and gives a lot of meaning to one's life. Check out the National Association of Student Cooperatives <nasco.coop> and the International Communities Directory <http://directory.ic.org> for community resources and information.

6.15 - Sex, Masturbation, and Pornography

Sex[A] and masturbation both have similar effects on the body by releasing the happy chemicals serotonin and dopamine *(Sperm)*. On the one hand, sex has the perks of creating great happiness, validating your physical qualities, and potentially bonds you more strongly to a person you love. On the other, sex comes with risks such as pregnancy, sexually transmitted diseases, and other emotionally difficult things like jealousy. Because it can deeply hurt you and the person involved, sex is not an ideal coping mechanism. It can, however, be nice as part of a relationship or connecting with someone.

Masturbation is a safer avenue to orgasmic pleasure than sex because it is disease and pregnancy free. The main concern is the use of pornography as a masturbatory tool. Pornography can be part of a healthy masturbatory experience if consumed with full consciousness of what you are seeing, though that can be difficult. Mainstream porn has the tendency to promote unrealistic gender, relationship, and sexual roles and rarely represents how real sexual encounters occur. Dependency is also frequently a problem for depressed folks, and many people find themselves not just using porn, but needing to. Dependency on porn interferes with daily tasks, creates social anxiety, and can induce unhealthy thinking about yourself or others. If you think your porn use meets these criteria it might be a good idea to put the porn away and work on

---

A   Safe and consensual only please!

exploring your body without masturbation aids (or with different ones). Seek therapy if this is a struggle, or download porn blocking software and set a random password you won't remember. There are also alternatives to mainstream porn, such as "feminist porn," which promote healthier views on sex and the people involved.

6.16 - Celebrate Changes

Suffering sometimes stems from disliking changes in life, for instance the change of seasons, growing older, the loss of a loved one, moving, or a medical operation. Rather than having these changes suddenly consume your life, meet them halfway and celebrate. Throw a party, go on a hike, hold a ritual, meditate, have a bonfire, shout and scream at the top of a mountain, or anything that provides a release for you. This can be done alone but is especially nice with a group of people who benefit from the celebration of change too. For more information see *Rituals* (Section 6.1).

7
Taking Care of
Your Mind and Body

By taking care of your mind and body, you will be healthier now and happier with your health later. Your mind and body are one. Chemicals from the brain direct the body, and what you do to and put into your body alters the chemical composition of the brain. Chemicals such as serotonin, dopamine, and norepinephrine have a huge impact on mood. It must be noted that there are people born with chemical and genetic abnormalities that prevent these and other chemical processes from happening naturally. People may also develop abnormalities during their lifetime, but normally you can influence these mood-altering chemicals with how you treat yourself through eating, exercising, sleeping, and taking supplements and medicines (Chapter 8).

7.1 - Food

Poor diet has been linked to depression and anxiety *(Poor)*. For me, eating a certain way affects my mood within a short period of

time. If I eat a lot of something like bread or sugar, I will have no desire to be around people because I feel agitated and anxious. Poor diet is the result of both not consuming the right foods and consuming the wrong foods. Depending on your body type, age, and ethnicity, you may need a slightly different diet than others, but there are general guidelines to healthy eating:

- Always stay hydrated. Try forming a habit of drinking water when you wake up, throughout the day, and whenever you start feeling hungry.
- Make time to have breakfast and a mid-morning snack, both of which have been shown to improve mood *(Smith, Andrew P. and Amanda Wilds)*.
- Consume a wide assortment of both cooked and raw whole foods with a variety of colors. If this is difficult to afford try growing vegetables in a garden or pots.
- Forgetting to eat or irregular eating may cause periods of low blood sugar, resulting in irritation, stress, and tiredness.
- Avoid heavily processed foods which lack nutrients such as chips and candy, and, if possible, eat from local and organic

farms you know are not using toxic pesticides and herbicides.

- Some foods such as lima beans are healthy but bind nutrients and must not be eaten all the time.

- Maintaining healthy gut bacteria by regularly consuming prebiotic[A] supplements and probiotic foods such as yogurt and sauerkraut help reduce stress (*Gregoire*).

- See a nutritionist to help you figure out if you're missing anything or need help creating a wholesome diet. You can also create a nutrient profile for yourself by recording information from food labels and going to websites like *The World's Healthiest Foods* <www.whfoods.com/foodstoc.php> and *Self Nutrition Data* <http://nutritiondata.self.com>.

- There is a lot of information and misinformation about diet so check multiple sources and keep biases from places such as food corporations in mind.

- Some scientists associate depression with inflammation, so consuming anti-inflammatory foods such as berries, onions, garlic, broccoli, apples, almonds, olive oil, turmeric, anti-oxidant rich foods, and foods with omega-3 fatty acids such as fish may improve your mood (*Kresser; Siple*).

Exclusion Diets

Along with eating nutritious foods, you might also consult a nutritionist about going on an exclusion diet to see how different foods allergically affect you. Many physical and mental conditions may be caused by reactions to certain foods, even if you have eaten those foods for your whole life. My friends and I have seen altering the way we eat affect our skin conditions, anxiety, and energy levels. Going on an exclusion diet means removing a common allergen such as wheat, dairy, corn, and soy from your diet and replacing it with a typically less allergenic substitute such as quinoa, rice, or

---

A   Prebiotics are substances that support the growth of beneficial bacteria.

almond milk. Avoid consuming processed foods during this time because many are packaged in the same facility as or contain derivatives of a food you are avoiding. After several weeks without the commonly allergenic food, note any changes you experienced and see how you react to eating the food again; if your symptoms are the same your nutritionist may recommend repeating this process with another allergen. The results can be very surprising! See the "Allergy Exclusion Diet" page on <WHFoods.org> for more information.

Eating Intentionally

Some people experience depressed feelings surrounding unintentional eating, such as overeating or snacking due to constant food cravings. Here are some ideas for bringing more intention to eating and changing habits surrounding food consumption:

- According to Wiktionary the word "breakfast," actually means "to break the nightly fast" *(Breakfast)*. In the morning say "I break my nightly fast" before beginning to eat to acknowledge that you are now eating.

- Brush your teeth after each meal, this will wash flavors from your mouth that might create food cravings later. For me a clean mouth makes random snacking less desirable.

- Eat as many meals as possible with other people at scheduled times.

- Set an alarm between meals, eating at specific times each day.

- If you are gifted food you are trying to avoid, you don't have to eat it. Regifting or composting is better than putting detrimental foods into your body.

- Form a habit of filling a bowl or plate with as much food as you think you'll want to eat and still feel good afterward. Even if you still feel hungry, do not return for seconds until you give yourself at least half an hour to ensure you actually are.

- Eat slowly, focusing wholly on the flavor and texture of the food as well as the feelings in your stomach. No talking or thoughts, just mindfully experiencing the sensations. Stop when you feel full.
- Only buy whole foods that have not been heavily processed.
- Consider the amount of money saved by not buying "junk" foods or ready to eat meals.
- Say a prayer or give thanks for the food you are eating before you eat it.
- When you feel hungry drink water before eating food. Sometimes feelings of hunger, especially when you have recently eaten, is a sign of dehydration.
- Grow some of your own food to see how much work goes into its creation.
- Do work away from the kitchen or outside of the house. Store food in cabinets or in the fridge to keep it out of sight.
- If you eat as a result of stress, a habit cue, try forming a parallel habit of breathing deeply when stressful sounds or situations arise. Over time you may be able to stop compulsively eating and start compulsively deep breathing and meditating.
- To prevent food cravings stay away from places that food is being cooked in or that smell strongly of food.
- Contrary to the idea that eating everything on your plate is saving food, overeating[A] is actually another form of food waste. Save money and your stomach by refrigerating leftovers for tomorrow's meal or turning them into compost for a garden bed or flower pot.

A   Eating more than your body type and activity levels require, or eating until you feel uncomfortably full.

7.2 - Nutrients, Malabsorption, and Genetics

Depression is a common symptom of nutrient deficiency *(Davison K Michelle)*. In one study, most subjects diagnosed with bipolar or severe depression were found to lack one or more of the following: fiber, α-linolenic (omega-3 fatty acid) and linoleic acid (omega-6 fatty acid), the B vitamins including thiamin (vitamin B1), riboflavin (vitamin B2), niacin (vitamin B3), pantothenic acid (vitamin B5), vitamin B6 (pyridoxine), folate (vitamin B9), and vitamin B12, vitamin C, calcium, magnesium, potassium, iron, phosphorus, and zinc. Nearly all of these vitamins and minerals are well established in maintaining healthy brain function. Other nutrients that play a role in mood and depression include vitamin D and selenium (see the nutrient table at the end of this section).

In the United States most people base their nutrient intake on recommended daily allowances (RDAs). The RDAs seen on food packaging are the recommended minimum nutrient intake of vitamins and minerals to be healthy, which means you can take more of most nutrients without negative side effects. It is rare to get too much of a nutrient by eating whole foods, but if you begin taking supplements, follow the serving sizes and directions to prevent overdosing. A wholesome diet with lots of variety will get you most of the nutrients you need to be healthy, but food and how each individual's body processes it is complex, so deficiencies may still arise. Furthermore, nutrients from fruit and vegetables are dependent upon the soil they are grown in. **A deficiency in the soil means a deficiency in the food grown.** If possible, get to know your local farmer and ask them how they grow your food. It's for your health!

Any nutrient deficiency can cause problems, so consider having a medical professional test your nutrient levels. Unfortunately these tests are rarely covered by health insurance, but if you can afford $100 to $300, ask your doctor where you can take one. The nutritionist may instruct you to supplement with a multivitamin or eat more of certain foods.

Note that fortifying nutrients you are deficient in after a nutrient test may not be enough. Several genetic conditions and diseases cause malabsorption and prevent your body from optimal mental and physical health. Therefore a second nutrient test or genetic testing is necessary to know if these nutrients are being absorbed properly. Genetic testing is sometimes necessary because a nutrient test will show the body having plenty of a nutrient, but it won't be using the nutrient at all. For instance, folate, or vitamin B9, may not be processed into its usable form, L-methylfolate, due to a genetic abnormality, and in turn heightens the potential for experiencing depression *(Nelson)*. With this condition a person may be consuming adequate levels of vitamin B9 but their body cannot use it. Once diagnosed by a medical professional, individuals may be given an L-methylfolate supplement.

Seasonal Affective Disorder: Vitamin D, Sunlight, and the Outdoors

A low level of vitamin D is often associated with seasonal affective disorder (SAD). SAD is a form of depression caused when a person does not get enough vitamin D, often during the winter months. A person can become vitamin D deficient any time of the year by not getting outside enough, or by wearing too much sunscreen or clothing. Skin color also affects the body's uptake of vitamin D with lighter skinned people absorbing more. The Office of Dietary Supplements recommends exposure to the outside for 5-30 minutes at least twice per week to absorb enough of the nutrient when sunlight is available, and for people with darker skin to supplement when there is little sunlight *(Dietary)*. Vitamin D does store up in the body, so it is possible with enough fall, spring, and summer sun exposure to last through a cloudy or shut-in winter, but more than likely you will have to supplement or consume vitamin D rich foods.

Vitamin D is actually a hormone that exists in two forms, D2 and D3 *(Crowther)*. In food D2 comes from plants like sunflower seeds, leafy greens, avocados, and carrots, and D3 comes from animal sources like mackerel, herring, salmon, liver, and lanolin (sheep's wool oil is often used as a D3 supplement). D3 is the same molecule synthesized when skin is exposed to sunlight. Because D2 must become D3 in the body, D2 is only utilized one-third as well as D3 *(Laura)*. To supplement, you can buy liquid drops, pills, or get a shot. Consuming fish oil is another option and includes omega-3 fatty acid.

The skin synthesizes vitamin D when struck with UVB rays from the sun *(Holick)*. However, UVB rays only penetrate the atmosphere when the sun is at certain angles. In places with a latitude above 37 degrees, UVB rays normally do not reach Earth's surface during the winter months. Even during the summertime in these areas, UVB rays only pass through between the hours of 10:00 AM and 3:00 PM, so be sure to expose yourself to the sun during these times.

Omega-3 and Omega-6 Fatty Acids

Maintaining a one-to-one ratio of omega-3 fatty acids to omega-6 fatty acids can greatly improve one's health by reducing the risk of "cardiovascular disease, cancer, and inflammatory and autoimmune diseases." *(Simopoulos)*. This ratio may also aid in preventing depression, though several studies report contrasting findings *(Logan)*. The important thing to consider though is that most people in the United States get far too much omega-6 fatty acids which come from things like corn oil, safflower oil, sunflower oil, and canola oil *(World's. omega-3 fatty acids)*. Sources of omega-3 fatty acids include flax seed, fish, walnuts, and soybeans *(World's. omega)*. It is heat sensitive, so you must eat foods containing omega-3 fatty acids raw and use oils containing them that are cold-pressed. It is also better absorbed in whole foods rather than in a supplemental form.

B Vitamins

Deficiency of B Vitamins, especially vitamin B12 and vitamin B9 (folate), is associated with depression *(Willamson)*. B12 only reliably comes from animal products, but some foods such as nutritional yeast are generally supplemented with it. Sources of B12 include liver, fish, beef, lamb, yogurt, and eggs *(World's. vitamin B12)*. Many people are B12 deficient even if they eat meat, because B12 "slowly loses its activity when exposed to light, oxygen, and acid or alkali-containing environments..." and is lost in water or meat juices during cooking due to its water solubility *(Kwak)*. Vitamin B9, also known as folic acid, or folate, comes from "romaine lettuce, spinach, asparagus,

RIBOFLAVIN ·· VITAMIN B12

turnip greens, mustard greens, calf's liver, parsley, collard greens, broccoli, cauliflower, beets, and lentils" *(World's. folate).*

Zinc

A deficiency in zinc can cause depression, so ensuring you are taking adequate levels is important *(Levenson).* Preliminary studies have shown an increased antidepressant effect by combining zinc supplementation with pharmaceutical antidepressants. Zinc has also been used alone to treat depression and mania *(Davison, Karen M.).* Good sources of zinc include meat, seeds, legumes, oats, and yogurt *(World's. Zinc).*

Selenium

Fortifying your selenium intake can improve mood *(Benton).* Depending on the soil quality, selenium may or may not be in foods like meat, fish, eggs, Brazil nuts, mushrooms, and mustard seeds *(World's. Selenium).*

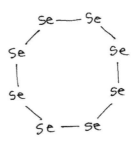

SELENIUM

Calcium

Too much or too little calcium can cause depression *(Arasteh).* Too little calcium limits normal brain function and absorption of vitamin D, while too much disrupts magnesium absorption, another mineral which helps prevent depression *(Harrison).* The balance involves consuming roughly equal or more amounts of magnesium than the RDA of calcium. Calcium is naturally found in dairy products, tofu, sesame seeds, collard greens, as well as spinach *(World's. calcium).* Most non-dairy milks are calcium fortified as well.

Nutrients to Fortify for Depression

*Please read the previous notes in conjunction with this list.

Nutrient:	Sources:
Vitamin B1 (thiamine), vitamin B2 (riboflavin), vitamin B6 (pyridoxine)*(Gardiner)*.	Liver, fish, dairy, chicken, potatoes, beans, dark leafy greens *(American)*, wheat bran *(Busch)*.
Vitamin B9 (folate)	"Romaine lettuce, spinach, asparagus, turnip greens, mustard greens, calf's liver, parsley, collard greens, broccoli, cauliflower, beets, and lentils" *(World's. Folate)*.
Vitamin B12	Liver, fish, beef, lamb, yogurt, eggs, nutritional yeast *(World's vitamin B12)*.
Vitamin C *(Zhang)*	Peppers, strawberries, broccoli, pineapple, brussels sprouts, kiwifruit, oranges, kale *(World's. vitamin C)*.
Calcium	Dairy products, tofu, sesame seeds, collard greens, spinach *(World's. Calcium)*.
Vitamin D2 (from plant sources)	Sunflower seeds, leafy greens, avocados, carrots *(Crowther)*.

Vitamin D3 (from animal sources and sunlight)	Sunlight, mackerel, herring, salmon, liver *(Crowther)*.
Iron *(Davison K Michelle)*	Beans, spinach, liver, venison, sesame seeds, olives *(World's Iron)*.
Magnesium *(Arnstein)*	Spinach, chard, soybeans, sesame seeds, black beans, quinoa, sunflower seeds, cashews *(World's. Magnesium)*.
Phosphorus *(Davison K Michelle)*	Meat, eggs, dairy products, nuts, legumes, whole grains, potatoes, garlic *(Phosphorus)*.
Potassium *(Davison K Michelle)*	Swiss chard, bananas, potatoes, yams, spinach, beans *(World's. Potassium)*.
Omega-3 Fatty Acid	Flax seed, fish, walnuts, and soybeans *(World's. Omega)*.
Selenium	Meat, fish, eggs, Brazil nuts, mushrooms, and mustard seeds *(World's. Selenium)*.
Zinc	Meat, seeds, legumes, oats, yogurt *(World's. Zinc)*.

7.3 - What Substances to Avoid

Note that there are no absolutes in terms of how any individual will react to a substance. Decreasing or removing the following items might lower the chance of experiencing depression for some, but will have no impact on others. As stated previously, just be mindful of how each substance makes you feel after consuming them, or, consider excluding them from your diet for a period of time.

Sugar

Refined sugar may cause or increase the risk of depression in some persons, especially women with lactose intolerance *(Deans)*. Regular consumption of sugar also reduces the effectiveness of receptors tied to producing serotonin *(Darakhshan 5)*. Everything has sugar in it, but the point is to avoid concentrated sugars such as in candy, sweet baked goods, soda, and some processed foods. This is especially important with the growing epidemic of type 2 diabetes, a completely preventable disease. A good alternative to processed sugars is fresh or dried fruit.

Cigarettes and Coffee(?)

In one study the use of cigarettes and coffee together were related to an increased chance of suicide in bipolar disorder patients *(Ross)*. Nicotine is also associated with causing episodes of schizophrenia in people who are predisposed to the condition, so it might be something that you choose to avoid *(Coulston)*. Then again, smoking is a

way to socialize and get outside, but comes with drawbacks to your health. Consider finding alternative means of getting these benefits in your day-to-day life.

Caffeine

Research shows an uncertain effect of caffeine on depression and anxiety. On one hand many studies have found that drinking a few cups of coffee a day improves mood *(Smith, Andrew P.)*. However, fur-ther studies on the direct chemical effect of caffeine reveal some troubling results. First, long term intake of the stimulant has been associated with a decrease in serotonin available for the body to use, even though serotonin levels increase *(B.S. Gupta 21)*. For people taking pharmaceutical drugs, caffeine also interacts with some of the same receptors and may prevent the drugs from taking their full effect *(Carrillo)*. Lastly, irregular consumption of caffeine can induce anxiety, such as only drinking a cup of coffee every couple of days *(Childs E)*. Common things containing caffeine include coffee, soda pop, tea, chocolate, and yerba mate. See Section 7.4 on sleep deterrents if you need an alternative to help you wake up, or simply consume beverages with less caffeine such as green tea.

Marijuana (Illegal)

In a comparison of studies, research showed that for some people medical marijuana can reduce or stop symptoms of depression and anxiety, while for others, medical marijuana makes depression worse *(procon.org)*. Many peer-reviewed studies associate heavy marijuana use with causing depression and anxiety *(Degenhardt)*. Heavy use of marijuana can also increase the chance of experiencing psychosis or having a schizophrenic episode *(Cohen)*. However, this may be dependent upon the strain of marijuana used. Either way, even medical marijuana does not currently cover depression as a condition it treats.

Alcohol

Alcohol has some downsides beyond hangovers and black-outs. Increased levels of alcohol consumption causes heightened levels of depression when sober *(Gail)*. Drinking alcohol while taking certain medications is also not suggested because it can change how the medications interact with your mind and body. In practice it is difficult to avoid alcohol in some social circles and can be very helpful for gaining the courage to meet new people and make friends. If you don't want to give up alcohol the best thing to do is to limit your consumption and be aware that symptoms of depression after sobering up may be caused by alcohol. Another option is to find alternative ways to be comfortable in social situations, such as with deep breathing, keeping busy preparing food, playing a game, or finding friends or communities that do not rely on substances to have fun. Like most other mind-altering substances, consuming alcohol to avoid emotions and thoughts is not healthy and will not help with getting better.

If you want help with limiting or stopping your alcohol consumption, consider joining a supportive community. Being able to work together with others who relate to your suffering can be a very powerful way to heal. The best known program is Alcoholics Anonymous <www.aa.org>. Different A.A. chapters have varying levels of spirituality involved in them. For those who do not want that aspect of A.A., there is also "Secular Organizations for Sobriety" (S.O.S.). S.O.S. shares a directory of alcohol and narcotics support groups which use a secular model of assistance <www.sossobri-ety.org>. For family and friends of alcoholics, the support groups "Al-Anon" or "Alateen" may be able to help. If groups are not your thing, seeing a therapist is another helpful outlet.

Narcotics

Any narcotic, especially if used extensively or regularly, will create depressive feelings when you are coming down from its effects. Assistance for those dealing with addictions to narcotics can be found through "Narcotics Anonymous" <m.na.org> or the previously mentioned "Secular Organizations for Sobriety."

Inflammatory Substances

Some scientists believe that depression is an inflammatory reaction, thus consuming inflammatory substances may increase the potential of experiencing a depressive episode (*Kresser*). Certain medications and foods cause inflammation. Common inflammatory foods include oils high in omega-6 fatty acids, trans fats, saturated fat from meat and dairy, sugar, refined grains such as white bread and pasta, alcohol, and gluten (*Klein*).

Pollutants

Exposure to certain substances such as lead can cause genetic, hormonal, chemical, or neurological abnormalities. Some people also experience chemical sensitivity and adverse effects from the toxins found in nearly all consumer products, the air, and foods. In one study, workers moved from a conventional office building into a 'green' office building built with natural materials and better natural lighting. The business experienced increased productivity as fewer people were absent due to depression, asthma, stress, and respiratory allergies *(S Korkmaz)*. Mold and dampness can cause depression as well, so if your home has these problems, consider

using a dehumidifier *(M Brown)*. Keeping a window open to filter in fresh air will also help decrease a buildup of pollutants and disease-causing pathogens *(Jessica)*. Be conscientious of the toxins found within paint, shampoo, clothing, food, and construction materials like insulation. There are a number of plants that filter out airborne pollutants within a living space. According to NASA, the following list is comprised of the best plants for filtering air pollutants *(Richard)*.

Best Air-Filtering Plants

- English Ivy (Hedera helix).
- Spider plant (Chlorophytum comosum).
- Golden pothos or devil's ivy (Scindapsus aures or Epipremnum aureum).
- Peace lily (Spathiphyllum 'Mauna Loa').
- Chinese evergreen (Aglaonema modestum).
- Bamboo palm or reed palm (Chamaedorea sefritzii).
- Snake plant or mother-in-law's tongue (Sansevieria trifasciata 'Laurentii').

- Heartleaf philodendron (Philodendron oxycardium, syn. Philodendron cordatum).
- Selloum philodendron (Philodendron bipinnatifidum, syn. Philodendron selloum).
- Elephant ear philodendron (Philodendron domesticum).
- Red-edged dracaena (Dracaena marginata).
- Cornstalk dracaena (Dracaena fragans 'Massangeana').
- Janet Craig dracaena (Dracaena deremensis 'Janet Craig').
- Warneck dracaena (Dracaena deremensis 'Warneckii').
- Weeping Fig (Ficus benjamina).
- Gerbera Daisy or Barberton Daisy (Gerbera jamesonii).
- Pot Mum or Florist's Chrysanthemum (Chrysantheium morifolium).
- Rubber Plant (Ficus elastica).

Many of these are common household plants and can be found at your local plant nursery. Another option to being surrounded by plants is moving to the countryside.

7.4 - Sleeping and Awakening

There is no exact amount of sleep any individual needs, although too much or too little sleep is associated with several health problems *(How Much)*. A healthy amount of sleep for adults is 7 to 9 hours per day, for teenagers 8.5 to 9.25 hours per day, and 5 to 10 year-olds 10 to 11 hours per day. Keep in mind that tiredness can act as a trigger for negative feelings from not sleeping enough, sleeping too much, eating certain foods, or by performing physically and mentally strenuous activities. Listen to your body and allow it the amount of rest it really needs.

Sleep Aids

- Take a natural sleep aid such as chamomile, melatonin, or valerian.
- Avoid viewing electronic media within a few hours before sleep. The screen interacts with your brain in such a way that it makes your sleep less restful and makes it more difficult to fall asleep *(Trapani)*.
- Exercising in the morning or midday helps with falling asleep later, but don't exercise at night; it makes falling asleep harder *(Trapani)*.
- Foods such as warm milk, bananas, potatoes, oatmeal, and whole-wheat bread help induce sleep *(Trapani)*.
- Make sleeping a routine with brushing your teeth, flossing, changing into pajamas, and maybe a small activity as part of it. Go to bed and wake up at the same time each day, and only use your bed for sleeping and sex, not working in. By using a routine like this, your body will know it is time to sleep *(Smith, Melinda)*.

- Only nap earlier in your day and keep naps to below 30 minutes *(Smith, Melinda)*.
- Only expose yourself to dim light when you're ready for bed to allow the level of melatonin, the natural sleep hormone, to increase and tell the body it is time to sleep *(Smith, Melinda)*. Note that the light from a full moon diminishes your quality of sleep and makes it harder to fall asleep as well *(Cajochen)*.
- Make your bedroom a comfortable space by eliminating noises, keeping it dark, and maintaining a temperature of 65 degrees Fahrenheit or below *(Smith, Melinda)*.
- Don't eat big meals, drink large amounts of liquids, or consume alcohol late at night. Smoking at all or drinking caffeine a few hours past when you wake up both make it harder to sleep and diminish your quality of sleep *(Smith, Melinda)*.
- Eat enough that you don't get hungry at night.
- Stress can prevent you from sleeping *(Smith, Melinda)*. Sometimes when I can't sleep or am obsessing over a thought, going into a state of meditation and only focusing on deep breathing helps me fall asleep.
- If you wake up in the middle of the night, worrying about being able to fall back asleep will only keep you awake *(Smith, Melinda)*. Try to relax thoughtlessly or do a calm activity such as reading for a little while.
- Avoid putting disturbing or stressful things in your mental scope such as horror movies. At least for myself, these stimuli increase the chance that I have nightmares and diminish my quality of sleep. Not only that, but also once experienced, they stay with you for the rest of your life. Be considerate of what you want your memories to be composed of.

- Nightmares can be a source of poor sleep. It is especially important to deal with nightmares because good dreams provide a deeper sense of rest and possible insight or healing. Often what you experience and think about during your waking hours seeps into your dreams, so first try removing easily avoidable negative stimuli from your life such as horror movies and world news media. Working through other negative stimuli such as trauma or changing how you think and perceive the world around you may help as well. To directly gain better control of dreams, write your dreams down. Keep a notebook and pen next to your bed and jot dreams down as soon as you wake up. You can also alter your dreams by focusing on what you want to dream about as you fall asleep. Focusing on dreaming will also help you remember your dreams when you wake up. For more information on gaining control of your dreams, look into guides on lucid dreaming.

- Listen to soothing recorded background sounds like rain, wind, and ocean waves to help mask or block out noises that keep you awake. You can find noise generating applications online and for smart phones. You can also turn on a fan, or wear earplugs if they aren't too uncomfortable for your ears.

Sleep Deterrents

- Eat foods that contain protein and fat along with carbohydrates and sugar. Eating fruit or carbohydrates like bread alone will increase your energy short term and then create a sugar crash, causing tiredness *(Newitz)*.

- If you use an alarm clock, set it away from your bed so you have to get up to turn it off.

- Exercise and stretch for 5 to 10 minutes, or longer, right after you wake up. This pairs nicely with mindfulness practices. In the short term doing the exercises will wake your body up, in the longer term your body will associate waking up with being prepared for activity.

- Get a consistent amount of sleep each night and don't oversleep.
- Expose yourself to lots of light, preferably direct sunlight, in the morning to lower levels of the natural sleep hormone, melatonin *(Smith, Melinda)*.
- Try to get outside and moving within an hour of waking up.
- Drink tea or coffee (note that some people crash several hours after drinking a caffeinated beverage).
- Shower in the morning instead of at night.
- Eat a more nutritious diet.
- Keep windows open or get outside throughout the day. The build up of CO_2 in a room with no airflow can cause drowsiness *(Carbon)*.

7.5 - Physical Activity

According to Dr. Mike Evans, exercise decreases the severity of depression by thirty to fifty percent *(Evans)*. Thirty minutes to an hour a day of activities like walking, cycling, swimming, or weight lifting can do more than prevent depression, they reduce pain in knee arthritis and the chance of hip fracture in post-menopausal women, reduce the progression into dementia and Alzheimer's, and reduce the risk of diabetes, heart disease, high blood pressure, death, and anxiety. Exercise is also the number one treatment for fatigue, and in  general improves one's quality of life. Thus, exercise may also relieve or stop depression associated with existing health problems. Change activities if you begin experiencing pain, but even if you feel fatigued all the time, exercise will only make your body stronger. I've found it helpful to start the morning right after I wake up in bed with a 10 minute combination of stretches, exercise, and mindfulness meditation.

If you have trouble motivating yourself to exercise, get a friend to go with you. Another option is becoming a dog owner to create a sense of obligation to get them outside. Pets also make great friends! If you have trouble finding time to exercise, do stretches while cooking, or lift weights watching television. Other energetic outbursts may be helpful as well such as singing, gardening, or making art.

8
Medicines for Depression and Anxiety

Reminder: I am not a medical professional. If you decide to use one of these substances prior to consulting with a medical professional, you do so at your own risk.

Pharmaceutical, psychedelic, and herbal medicines have been found to help relieve depression in users. Only an overview of taking pharmaceuticals is given in this guide, as a medical health professional should prescribe you the proper type and dosage for your needs. Although some herbal medicines are generally known to be safe, medical advice from an herbalist and doctor should be sought before regularly taking any herb in high doses. What I've included is an overview that will enable you to do further research. Due to the illegality of psychedelics, only preliminary research from doctors given special government approval is available. Recent research has included studies on LSD, ketamine (cat tranquilizers), psilocybin (magic mushrooms), and ecstasy.

8.1 - Pharmaceuticals and Doctor Prescribed Drugs

Pharmaceutical antidepressants and anti-anxiety medications can be very helpful for people that experience chronic genetic or chemical abnormalities in their body. When these abnormalities cause depression, they often result in major or severe depression. Pharmaceutical medicines correct the balance of chemicals or make up for malfunctioning genes.

I am not a medical professional, but from my research and conversations with people who do take antidepressants, this is what I understand about them: pharmaceuticals do sometimes work and can be of great help, but there is a problem with how many doctors prescribe them. The beginning of this book mentioned that, when pharmaceutical antidepressants do work, it is not well understood why. This is in part because doctors rarely test for the specific genetic abnormality or chemical deficiencies they are treating. As a result most doctors use a "guess and check" method when prescribing medications for depression and anxiety. Due to this lack of testing, as well as there being depression unrelated to chronic chemical and genetic abnormalities such as that caused by life experiences, life choices, and nutrient deficiencies, doctors may incorrectly prescribe pharmaceutical medicines. This is further exasperated by doctors rarely prescribing healthy life choices and coping mechanisms instead of, or alongside of, medications.

Even when you are correctly prescribed to take pharmaceutical antidepressants, you may need to try several different medications, the dosage may need to be adjusted, or you may need to take several antidepressants together to have a beneficial effect. Antidepressants can seemingly work for a short time and then stop working. Also keep in mind that it can take four or more weeks to feel any beneficial changes from a new medication.

Pharmaceutical antidepressants can cause a number of wide-ranging side effects as well. If you feel like the trade-offs are too much, become more depressed, or think of suicide, talk to your doctor. They may suggest a different medication, pair your current medication with another, or try a completely different method of controlling your depression. Switching medications can be very difficult emotionally, so try to have a solid support network to help you through your transition. If you want to get off your medication(s), talk to your doctor first to set up a schedule to slowly reduce your dosage; doing so too suddenly can result in symptoms of withdrawal such as heightened levels of depression. Whatever you decide to do, just remember that while medicines may be able to treat the root source of your depression, a content and happy life still relies on healthy habits and lifestyle choices.

8.2 - Herbal Medicines for Depression

5-HTP

5-HTP is a precursor to serotonin and is derived from the African plant, Griffonia simplicifolia *(Griffonia)*. There is very little research complete and no long-term studies. Short-term studies indicate 5-HTP is more effective than placebo controls in elevating mood *(Shaw)*. My personal experience has been positive, but I have always taken it in conjunction with Vitamin D3. 5-HTP is available online and through health food stores.

Lavender

Researchers found that lavender petal tea and extract helps lessen symptoms of depression *(Dwyer)*. It also smells great!

Marijuana(?) (Illegal)

As mentioned previously in the *What Substances to Avoid* (Section 7.3), marijuana can cause depression, anxiety, and even schizophrenia for some, but helps reduce depressive symptoms for others. Using marijuana on a case-by-case basis when depressive flare ups occur may have a more positive role in preventing depression. Specific cultivars of marijuana may also differ in their psychological effects upon an individual. Of course, marijuana is still considered illegal by the federal government and most state governments, and depression is not a condition covered under current medical marijuana prescriptions.

Saffron

Saffron Crocus is a flower that is grown in many parts of the world to make the very expensive saffron spice from the stigma *(Crocus)*. In one study comparing the anti-depressants Prozac and Imipramine to saffron, saffron was more effective and tolerable *(Dwyer)*. The petals seem to have similar anti-depressant qualities to the stigma and may help make saffron a cost-effective option in the future. Until then, you could grow your own and dry them.

St. John's Wort

According to a book review of *St. John's Wort and Its Active Principles in Depression and Anxiety* by the British Journal of Clinical Pharmacology, St. John's Wort is an effective antidepressant *(Szabadi)*. It, however, cannot treat cases of severe depression *(Carpenter)*. It is an herb, but it is also a potent medicine, and **must not be mixed with other medicines** such as "certain classes of immunosuppressants, antivirals, anticoagulants and oral contraceptives..." *(Szabadi)*. Take note as well that it lessens the efficacy of other drugs, thus limiting who can use it *(Dwyer)*. It is suggested that, like any antidepressant, you ask a medical professional before use, especially if transitioning from another antidepressant. One side effect of taking St. John's Wort is becoming more sensitive to sunlight, so be sure to cover up!

Turmeric (Curcumin)

Limited testing has been done in India with curcumin as an antidepressant. Curcumin is a compound found in turmeric. Alone, curcumin showed comparable efficacy to Prozak, and when paired with Prozak further increased Prozak's efficacy as an antidepressant *(J Sanmukhani)*. Curcumin must be taken with black pepper or pepper extract to absorb properly *(Weil)*.

8.3 - Herbal Medicines for Stress and Anxiety

Ashwagandha

Ashwagandha is an adaptogen, an herb that helps reduce anxiety or stress-inducing conditions *(G. Singh)*. It also helps prevent ulcers and is an aphrodisiac.

Coffee(?)

As mentioned earlier in the section, *What Substances To Avoid* (Section 7.3), many studies show that coffee improves mood, but it creates a dependency and might cause anxiousness for some *(Smith, Andrew P.)*.

Ginseng

Ginseng is a plant whose root is used for a number of purposes. Some species of ginseng, including Panax (Korean ginseng), Eleutherococcus senticosus (Siberian ginseng), and Withania somnifera (Indian ginseng), have been documented in lowering stress levels *(Head)*.

Golden Root

Small studies of the plant Rhodiola rosea, or golden root, have shown that taking extracts of the plant cause a reduction in anxiety and mental fatigue and improvement in sleep quality *(Head)*.

L-Theanine (Tea)

Extracted from green and black teas, L-Theanine has been shown to lower anxiety without a sedative effect *(Head)*. A cup of tea contains about 20 milligrams of L-Theanine, but the studies cited used much more concentrated extracts of the pure chemical.

Motherwort

Motherwort has a sedative effect and can calm a racing heart *(Rezaei)*. It is therefore sometimes used for anxiety.

Tulsi (Holy Basil)

Tulsi, or Holy Basil, has traditionally been used in India to treat a whole host of aliments. Few studies have been conducted on humans, but animal research and traditional usage suggests it is "antimicrobial, adaptogenic, antidiabetic, hepatoprotective, anti-inflammatory, anti-carcinogenic, radioprotective, immunomodulatory, neuroprotective, and cardio-protective" *(E Singh)*. The adaptogenic properties specifically help with stress and anxiety.

Valerian

Valerian helps with anxiety and is a sedative for those having trouble sleeping *(Head 9-10)*. Numerous studies show that, in comparison to pharmaceutical equivalents, there are fewer side effects too.

Other Herbs for Anxiety and Sleeping

Because of the lack of solid research regarding them and because some have dangerous side-effects, I won't go into detail about more herbs. Many others do exist which carry some evidence in reducing anxiety and working as sleep aids. These include brahmi (Bacopa monniera), gotu kola (Centella asiatica), rain-of-gold (Galphimia glauca), German chamomile (Matricarie chamomilla), lemon balm (Melissa officinalis), passionflower (Passiflora incarnata), kava kava (Piper methysticum), hops (Humulus lupulus), blue skullcap (Scutellaria lateriflora), and jujabe (Ziziphus jujuba) *(Head 125)*. Several of these compare in effectiveness evenly with pharmaceutical equivalents, but with fewer side effects. Some are also toxic if taken over long periods of time or at high doses, so again, it's important to do your research or consult a medical professional.

8.4 - Psychedelics (Illegal)

Researchers have found that small doses of psychedelics such as LSD, ketamine (cat tranquilizers), and psilocybin ("magic" mushrooms) reduce symptoms of depression, anxiety, and obsessive compulsive disorder for months after use *(Brauser)*. The theory is that patients are given a new perspective to look through and may thereby find a way around their typical negative mood *(Cloud)*. Ceremonial use of psychedelics by native groups continues to happen today, but these substances are illegal according to federal law. People can and have lost their mind with the recreational use of psychedelics, and so further testing is still needed before the medical community accepts psychedelics as a treatment for depression. For the latest research on psychedelic substances go to <www.maps.org/>, or read more personal accounts and safety issues at <www.erowid.org>.

8.5 - Ecstasy/MDMA (Illegal)

Past research (2004) indicates that the effects of Ecstasy/MDMA are negative, associating it with depression and delayed cognitive abilities *(C. Stough)*. However, more recent research (2012) that utilized better control techniques found that MDMA usage does not have long-term residual effects *(Szalavitz)*. In fact, after two or three MDMA aided therapy sessions, seventeen out of twenty patients suffering from post-traumatic stress disorder (PTSD) no longer showed symptoms associated with PTSD. This was with a controlled dosage in a controlled environment. Like most other "hard" drugs, outside of the lab many people do report having depressed feelings after the illegal usage of this substance. Even so, some have high hopes for MDMA-based therapy aiding in marriage counseling, PTSD, depression, schizophrenia, and more. Like most mind-altering drugs though, MDMA can be dangerous and is considered illegal by the federal government.

9
Thoughts for Change

Reforming my thinking patterns has been the most important aspect of cultivating happiness for myself. How I think about a situation often determines whether depressed feelings arise. Even if I am experiencing depression, certain thinking patterns can make those episodes much more tolerable or alleviate them altogether. Many practitioners of Buddhism believe that all humans have everything they already need to be happy regardless of their situation. I disagreed with this for a very long time, but now think it is possible, so long as a person has the right tools. These tools allow us to build up the parts of ourselves we like and break down the parts we want to move away from. In turn we cultivate happiness and contentment. This is not about avoiding or running away from difficult situations; it is about changing mental attitudes, unraveling mental distortions, and finding acceptance with our life story. The following chapter includes ways of thinking and changing thinking that I've found helpful. Keep in mind that just as you train your body to be stronger, the mind must also be given exercises and challenges to grow stronger. This takes time and energy, so don't get discouraged or overwhelm yourself. Grow one step at a time.

9.1 - Unmet Needs

Connecting your feelings to unmet needs will help put into perspective what causes you suffering and what actions to take in order to feel better in a given situation. Manfred Max-Neef believes that all humans have the same nine basic needs. Ask yourself if you are sufficiently receiving all these needs. If you are not, then figuring out how you can better meet these needs may help your situation. Reworded into simpler terms by Marshall Rosenberg, these needs are:

- Sustenance
- Safety
- Love
- Empathy
- Rest (recreation and play)
- Community
- Creativity
- Autonomy (freedom)
- Meaning (purpose)

(Nonviolent)

9.2 - Maintain a Positive Environment

Remove Negative Environments

It is important to have environments that nourish us because these spaces greatly influence our thoughts and feelings. Remove yourself from perpetually stressful or negative situations that you cannot confront or change. These might include a work environment or living situation. This is not the same as avoiding your emotions, but is rather a deep awareness of your feelings and needs. Creating huge changes can be difficult, but giving yourself the chance to be happy and comfortable is an essential baseline. You needn't see this as "running away" or "giving up," but rather as a healthy life decision. A negative space can be debilitating and make change nearly impossible.

Alter Your Daily Routine

Another option is to alter your daily routine by spending time in a different environment or doing something nice for yourself. Go to a friend's house, a park, a cafe, a pet spa, the farmers market, or the woods. Even if you can't get out, do something enjoyable like taking a hot bath, making a cup of tea, looking at pictures of cute animals, getting a massage, or meditating to cheer up. For me, changing my routine greatly relieves the stress built up by nit-picking the normal environments I engage in. Especially when I sleep in a different place, I realize that the world is much bigger than my normal scope of perception and my causes of stress suddenly become less important. Getting out to nature is especially relieving in that it is almost completely removed from humanity and city stresses such as noise and pollution. Just think about how the beauty of a forest or the ocean induce a calming state. For the sake of your mental health it is well worth your time to visit or live in environments like these.

Create Positive Living Spaces

Calmness is also manifested in aesthetic design, so organize and decorate your living and working spaces in such a way that it enhances your mood and makes you enjoy being there. If messes or difficulty finding things stress you out, clean up. You can also create an environment with colors, pictures, books, lighting, labels, quotes, order, and sounds that you find pleasing. In the end though, if an environment doesn't have the right feel, such as lacking an appropriate amount of natural light, you should consider moving or building your own home. For more ideas on making your space pleasant, read books or go online for information on feng shui, interior design, and organization.

Take Spatial Ownership

Even if a space is not yours to alter, you can mentally take ownership of it. Just observe the surrounding area from the floor to the ceiling and say, "I have a right to be here and a right to have my needs of safety and contentment met." It may seem like a strange thing to do, but this simple act creates a sense of empowerment by boosting confidence and comfort. Mind you, some spaces are not yours to be in and this should not be used as a means of over-staying your welcome.

Work as Play

Another mental trick is finding out how to see your work as play. Practicing mindfulness and being fully present with your work is a good starting point. Recognizing the needs that your work is meeting and being joyful for those needs being met is another. Work can be played as a game as well. How fast can you do a given task? Can you grow personally through exploring certain thoughts? Can you practice a skill? Can you listen to an informational audio recording? Can you find humor in what you have normally seen as mundane? There are many options for play.

9.3 - Collective Feelings

Sometimes many people, or a group of people, are simulta-neously stressed, sad, and feeling depressed. These collective feelings can "rub" off onto you, and make it all the more difficult to under-stand why you feel the way you do. There are multiple ways that col-lective feelings can spread. Stressful events such as college finals or a murder drive a community into a lower mood, in turn making that community express less positive attitudes in day-to-day interactions and social media.

Some people also contribute collective feelings to the phases of the moon and planetary cycles. There may be credibility to these beliefs. For instance, the light from a full moon interrupts the sleep hormone melatonin and in turn decreases deep sleep and makes fall-ing asleep more difficult (*Cajochen*). As discussed previously, sleep deprivation and low sleep quality increase the potential of experi-encing depressed feelings. If moonlight penetrates through your curtains, the best you can do is wear a sleeping mask, but exposure to the light of the moon during your evening hours may also con-tribute to melatonin disruption.

The experience of a collective mood is somewhat confusing with seemingly no trigger causing your depressed feelings. These collective feelings do tend to pass within several days. Just do what you can to maintain your self-care and be open with your commu-nity about the changes in your mood. It is gratifying to hear that everyone else you know experienced the same low.

9.4 - Stop Workaholism and Take Time for Yourself

Many people are brought up with an emphasis on efficiency and productivity doing work. However, it is important to realize that there are a number of ways to be efficient and productive, and one of those ways involves taking care of yourself. There is a balance to consider between being selfish and becoming overloaded with caring for others, but the point is to spend enough time caring for yourself to feel content and fulfilled. It may seem as though something awful will happen if you take a break from all the work you "need" to do, as if walls will crumble or some other catastrophe will occur, but this is very rarely true. Contentment and happiness become harder to grasp the less you care for yourself, and so it is important to take the time necessary to recharge and enjoy life.

Try scheduling one day a week that is absolutely your day. Plan the entire time around good self-care, and do nothing (even thinking) related to projects or work that have been put upon you. It may be hard at first, but undoing the learned behavior of over-working yourself and instead putting a priority on mental wellness is an important step to finding contentment in life. If one day is too much initially, try for half the day, or an hour each day. Another option is to go on a weekend adventure, or schedule time off for something longer. You deserve it.

9.5 - Therapy

Everyone and everything you ever meet will be a teacher, whether they guide you toward or away from the thoughts, activities, and experiences bountiful in the world. There is knowledge in all interactions, and we may seek it out through friendships, family, therapists, spiritual and religious teachers, support groups, dreams, horoscopes, and even pets.

Friends and Family

Have people in your life that you can talk to about your depression. Even if you don't feel like socializing, forcing yourself to be around people you enjoy can knock you out of a depressed state. More people than you think relate to how you're feeling and can assure you that the world is not falling apart. Keeping it bottled up will only make matters worse. That said, be careful with how much you ask of one person; it can be difficult for them as well. Spread out your friend base and try not to be negative all the time, or to continuously reiterate the same negative thoughts or happenings to one person. Once is enough, and more than that can be destructive to yourself as well as your friend. Use the support of friends to create positive spaces where you can safely have constructive dialogues and do fun activities. If your friends do not fulfill these needs when you are depressed, or your depression alienates your friends, seeing a professional therapist or support group may be for you. This act will allow you to process negative thoughts and feelings around a neutral figure while preserving time with friends and family for positive social interactions and experiences. See Section 6.14 for more information.

Professional Therapists

Professional therapists are trained to help you get to the root of your psychological difficulties, analyze why you are depressed, and confront those causes whether past or present. Although often expensive, some therapists have sliding scale fees for those with low income. Some insurance plans also cover therapy. Every therapist is different, so if one doesn't work for you, another might. Don't be afraid of switching therapists! Interview a new therapist to make sure that you feel comfortable speaking with them and that they are knowledgeable in the areas you want to work on. Unless you are having a crisis, it may be several weeks between beginning the process of searching for a therapist and working on your life with them. It is therefore beneficial to seek out a therapist while in a stable mood so you can immediately access help when in need. The paperwork you sign does revoke some of your confidentiality, but unless you are seriously considering suicide, going to harm someone, or a court asks for your files to be released, information you share with your therapist remains safe.

There are many different types of therapists, a number of which specialize in specific psychological conditions. A few types of therapy used for depressed persons include psychoanalysis, psychodynamic therapy, cognitive therapy, behavior therapy, interpersonal therapy, cognitive behavioral therapy (very popular), cognitive hypnotherapy, experiential therapy, and online therapy. Conduct research online or ask your doctor what type of therapy would best meet your needs.

Spiritual and Religious Teachers

Professional therapists, while often helpful, come from a scientific and institutional perspective that may lack a spiritual, religious, and cultural understanding of a person. Depending on your beliefs, some advice and healing is better found in spiritual and religious teachers. This therapy may take place one-on-one, in a congregation, in a group, in books or videos, or in a ceremony.

Support Groups

Support groups can greatly relieve stress and depression, especially when caused by physical ailments such as cancer or illness *(U Koc)*. Interacting with someone else who has been through the same difficulties as you makes the act of speaking openly about your symptoms, past, and emotions much easier. A good support group incorporates fun activities, goal setting, positive affirmations, and mutual support. Many support groups exist, and if they don't in your area you could start your own, or find ones that fit your needs online at sites like <psychcentral.com/resources/Depression/Support_Groups/>. There is also a twelve-step program for depression and depressed feelings called Emotions Anonymous <www.emotionsanonymous.org>. You are not alone in your struggles.

Dreams

Some of my most important healing, especially around trauma, has happened through dreaming. This came about by paying attention to my dreams, writing them down, and analyzing them. Read *Sleeping and Awakening* (Section 7.4) to learn how to deal with nightmares and gain better control of your dreams.

Horoscopes

Horoscopes provide material to help deepen your understanding of yourself. Based on planetary alignment, moon position, and your birth date, astrology is an alternative explanation of why things are the way they are in your life. Even if you don't believe in astrology or resonate with all of the horoscopes for you, many give advice that is good for anyone to follow and can be a fun thing to look forward to during the week. You could even read all the signs and choose which advice you want to take that week. My favorites are <www.freewillastrology.com> and <www.chaninicholas.com/>. If you want to look up your astrological chart, go to <astro.cafeastrology.com>.

Pets

Any type of pet is therapeutic to spend time with. Research has found that contact with an animal improves comfort, increases feelings of safety, decreases depression and anxiety, lowers blood pressure and stress, and even helps create trust between patients and medical professionals *(Jackson)*. Furthermore, pets help teach you about compassionate behavior, an essential skill for developing friendships. If you can't have your own cat, dog, horse, or the like, consider going to a pet spa or animal shelter to spend some time with those cute critters. There are also pet therapy programs with horses, or doctors can even prescribe you a cat for dealing with anxiety.

9.6 - Media Addiction and Staying in Tune with "Reality"

Media is a very powerful tool. Music, movies, books, news, cartoons, documentaries, video games, and so forth inspire thoughts, emotions, and experiences we may never have had otherwise. They give us heroes to look up to and allow us to see romanticized or condensed stories of lifestyles we may wish to embrace or strive for. Awareness of how these influences relate to our mental health is therefore important.

Consider the media and entertainment you voluntarily and involuntarily experience. Are you utilizing media in a destructive manner to make your mood worse? Going without media (no music, movies, fictitious books, etc) allows one to see a whole different side of life. If you try this, note how it makes you feel. What do you do with your time instead? I went five months without media and felt better than I ever had before. During that time I would only watch a movie or listen to music if others were experiencing it with me, which was rare. Afterward I no longer had the same addiction to media and entertainment, but could see, for instance, that music inspired me in certain situations and video games or television helped me cope when I really needed to stop thinking about something in a negative feedback loop. The break also gave me time to do more fulfilling things like make art and hang out with friends.

I have found that media can be an addiction that perpetuates an avoidance of emotions, thoughts, creativity, and healthy habits. While sometimes avoiding thoughts and feelings is healthy, it can also prevent getting better or fixing bad situations. For me, engaging in media too long makes my head foggy and in turn makes socializing with people really difficult. To remedy some aspects of this I began going to cafes to work on my computer or setting an alarm to take a break from media viewing.

News media can also consume your time and emotions to the point of preventing you from experiencing fulfillment in life. What do you really need to know about? Are you drowning in the depression of media sensationalism and propaganda when you could be caring for your local community and things you can actually change? You don't need that news! Once you realize what is beneficial to you and what is not, add back in those items and be wary of others.

Simultaneously, or instead of removing media from your life, study "media literacy." Studying media will help you understand the underlying messages presented, see biases, and question the authenticity of the information given. From here you can begin removing oppressive and demeaning media from your life, and substitute appropriate alternatives in their place.

In general, transform your hobbies into methods of self-care and pro-social behavior. Be conscious and selective of what you experience, because it all shapes who you are and what you think about. This may be difficult at first, but as you replace fiction with reality, life becomes its own exciting adventure story.

9.7 - Acceptance of Who You Are

Depression is often caused by health problems or feelings of inadequacy. It is important to realize that you are not alone feeling judged or not good enough. Within the United States of America almost everyone grows up with self-doubt over their perceived imperfections. This is because our media portrays images of perfection to strive for that are actually fictitious or unhealthy in nature. There are times when having self-doubt or being judged make sense, and it makes sense to improve your life in such a way that you no longer are judged or have a need to feel self-doubt. Most of the time though, ignoring those stigmas makes more sense, especially when you have no control over the part of yourself in question, or when it is an unhealthy part to change. In these cases, practicing mindfulness meditation and doing things that boost your self-esteem can help alleviate negative feelings. A good starting point is to befriend people who do not judge you and who accept your personal qualities. Another starting point is acknowledging that the majority of being able to do anything is simply believing in yourself and trying. Take small steps and do not expect perfection immediately. Thirdly, clarify any fuzzy ideologies or habits you might have by identifying who you want to be perceived as and cutting out the actions that contradict that person.

Remember that you are only who you are in this present moment, and that every new moment you have an opportunity to change. Your past selves have helped develop you into who you are now, but those people are no longer you. Sure the past happened, but it stops there, and is no longer happening. Sometimes just saying "I no longer need that memory," "I unbind myself from the past," or "YOLO (you only live once)" can be a powerful way of moving forward. Even just acknowledging in a room that it is your space and that nothing in that space from the past or future is happening can help get you out of your head. Take a moment to embrace and accept the person, the labels, and the interests you are now.

9.8 - Abundance Mentality and Fighting Regret

"When you catch yourself slipping into a pool of negativity, notice how it derives from nothing other than resistance to the current situation."

-Donna Quesada, *Buddha in the Classroom: Zen Wisdom to Inspire Teachers*

Another option of accepting who you are is to create an "abundance mentality" in your life *(Edberg)*. Think about the positive things as well as the possibilities of positive things in your life instead of what you do not, or cannot have. If you always complain about a certain time of your life, find good things that were happening then, or what good occurred because of difficulties during that time. You could also consider every new moment of your life an exciting adventure.

A lot of depression stems from ingrained thinking patterns. While it is difficult to alter learned behaviors, it is possible, and well worth it. You have the most power over how you feel, as well as the ability to deflect or reduce what you don't want to feel. An abundance mentality gives you a tool in which to help do this. For instance, if you are anxious about going to visit someone, say aloud, "I am excited to know this person better" or "I'm joyful to have these new experiences today." If a friendship or romance doesn't work out, you could say "I am glad for this new-found time to develop myself and cultivate more relationships" or "I learned so much while with that person."

Thinking something will make you feel bad will most certainly make you feel bad, just as in a self-fulfilling prophecy. However, if you maintain an open mind to how an event will impact your emotions, or see the positive possibilities available to you through such an event, the negative feelings will remain for much less time or not be there at all. Do not confuse this with avoiding feelings–when regrets or tragedies do arise, you fully experience the pain they cause, but then move forward and use them as an opportunity to learn and grow. By embracing an abundance mentality you simply become much more tolerant toward changes, whether people cancel plans on you or a difficult event happens in your life. Every moment is full of positive possibilities.

A wonderfully written, absurdly silly, and yet serious book to help you cultivate an abundance mentality is *Pronoia Is The Antidote for Paranoia* by Rob Brezsny. In one chapter Brezsny writes, "You came into this world as a radiant bundle of exuberant riddles. You slipped into this dimension as a shimmering burst of spiral hallelujahs. You blasted into this realm as a lush explosion of ecstatic gratitude. And it is your birthright to fulfill those promises"

(Brezsny 81). In another chapter he says "Thousands of things go right for you every day, beginning the moment you wake up. Through some magic you don't fully understand, you're still breathing and your heart is beating, even though you've been unconscious for many hours. The air is a mix of gases that's just right for your body's needs, as it was before you fell asleep" *(Brezsny 6)*. There are literally hundreds of questions, thoughts, and poems to wake you up to how amazing you, the world, and universe are.

9.9 - Fix Distorted Beliefs

Feelings	Thoughts/ Beliefs	Distortion(s)	Alternate Thought
Sad, angry, anxious.	I'm unlovable.	All-or-nothing thinking.	My relationship with this person did not work out.
	I really enjoyed my time with them.	Not a distortion.	I really enjoyed my time with them.
	I dislike everyone.	Disqualifying the positive and magnification.	I am upset with how some people treat me.

Cognitive therapy offers a useful tool for sorting out rational thoughts from distorted ones. Common distortions include "all-or-nothing thinking, overgeneralization, mental filter, disqualifying the positive, jumping to conclusions, magnification or minimization, emotional reasoning, should statements, labeling and mislabeling, and personalization" *(Schimelpfening)*. For more information on these, research "cognitive distortions." You can untangle distorted thinking by sorting out which thoughts and feelings are true and justified, and which need alteration. For a given situation the table above provides a useful framework to work from. This example situation involves the thoughts a person might have after being broken up with.

Once you realize an alternative or more reasonable thought, you can focus on that instead of the negative thought(s) you were having. You can also combine this technique with an abundance mentality to reform negative thoughts into ones which promote the positive aspects of a situation.

9.10 - Boost Confidence and Self-Esteem

Depressed feelings may be triggered by stressful events or the approach of events. When you have the time, prepare by boosting your confidence and self-esteem. According to researcher and 2012 TedGlobal speaker Amy Cuddy, using your body's natural power poses decreases anxiety and stress while simultaneously boosting your confidence and self-esteem *(Cuddy)*. Power poses include those that take up a lot of space. For instance, putting your hands on your hips, or even better, creating a victory stance by raising your hands up into the air and widening your legs. Doing so for just two minutes will have lasting effects, at least long enough to give your speech or attend that meeting. This technique may be more effective by getting really into the act. As Amy Cuddy says, "fake it till you make it!" For instance, look into the mirror and talk yourself up while in the pose, or play the part of a great orator. What will also help boost confidence and self-esteem, as well as help you play this role, is dressing in a way that makes you feel good about yourself. Pick clothing, a hairstyle, and makeup that is intentional and fits the situation. "Fake it till you make it" means that it's possible to use simple techniques like these until, over time, you aren't just faking confidence, you are more confident and you do have better self-esteem. Remember also that nothing will happen unless you first try, and as Marshall Rosenberg likes to say, "anything worth doing is worth doing poorly."

9.11 - Accept What You Fear

Many feelings are absolutely rational, but others create unnecessary strife and misdirect where action is needed. Underlying feelings such as hatred, dislike, and jealousy are sometimes fear. By identifying this root emotion you take responsibility for external or internal conflict and can challenge yourself to grow. There might be a fear of not being as good as someone else, being wrong, of a recurrence of a past event, being harmed, being emotionally hurt, or being embarrassed. For instance, if you have a problem keeping friends, becoming angry, walking around publicly, being intimate with a person, or seeing others being intimate, you can ask yourself how fear is influencing the feelings you experience when put in those situations. Which of these fears are rational and which are irrational? Which can you transform?

Accepting the outcomes of certain fears also allows us to move on and sprout happiness where once there was negativity. Many hobbies, habits, and thinking patterns result from the fear of what would happen if we did not do one thing or another. However, this creates a negative mindset when doing these things. Activities often pursued out of fear and negativity include activism, social tendencies, dressing up, diets, and careers. If your actions are based on fear, work on accepting the worst possible outcome of not doing that thing. Instead of holding onto the fear, allow it to fully happen in your imagination. Generally this outcome really isn't that bad, and at the very worst is only one of thousands of possibilities that could happen. Holding onto one possibility that makes you feel bad is simply not productive. It might be helpful to even stop doing the fear-based activity altogether for a little while. Transform negative tendencies into positive ones by pursuing those activities out of enjoyment, happiness, love, or fulfillment. If you cannot alter these feelings, pursue different activities.

9.12 - Make a Game

Throughout history people have played games because they are fun. Games bring an exciting dynamic to activities that make people try harder, work better, and enjoy it. Transforming mundane tasks into games will help you form habits and think more positively about the task that you're doing. You can form games with yourself or compete against other people. For instance, how fast can you fold the laundry, or guess how many pancakes of X size you can make with the amount of batter you've mixed, or try to beat your best mile time running, or spend a day without using certain words in your sentences. There is a game hidden in every corner of life.

9.13 - Losing and Finding Identity

Some people experience confusion and depression surrounding a loss of their identity. Identity crises may result from a changing of personality, aging, loss of loved ones, leaving a community or family, an injury or disease, changing environments, attempting to accommodate new friends or a new community, changing genders, or changing sexes. The loss of an identity may be thought of as an exciting opportunity to create an even better, stronger, and truer you, or simply to try out a different way of life. Time is a very important component of finding a new identity or re-finding an identity. It usually will not happen overnight, especially when friends and family try to reinforce your old patterns. It is therefore important to inform family and old friends of your changes, as well as to find new friends, community, and activities to engage in for support developing your new identity. For more information, see *Friendships, Relationships, and Community* (Section 6.14). It will also be helpful to explore yourself through writing, and even create a plan of what your new identity looks like. To move forward you might also need to release everything from the past and live wholly in the present moment, or hold a ritual or ceremony for your change (See Section 6.1).

A temporary form of identity loss known as disassociation also occurs when a person does not confront suffering in their life or is uncomfortable with themselves or a given situation. The individual is suddenly unsure of where they are, who they are, or who they are speaking with. It can last anywhere from several seconds to several hours. If you experience this form of identity loss, consider seeing a therapist, finding ways of accepting yourself, and confronting the sources of your suffering.

9.14 - Find Purpose and Meaning in Life

Viktor Frankl wrote in his book, *Man's Search For Meaning*, "...it is a characteristic of the American culture that, again and again, one is commanded and ordered to 'be happy.' But happiness cannot be pursued; it must ensue. One must have a reason to 'be happy'" *(Smith, Emily)*. In other words, happiness is nothing without first having a sense of meaning or purpose in one's existence. Happiness will come when you focus on living your life fully without avoiding negative emotions and circumstances.

Deciding on a specific purpose or passion can be a helpful grounding point to live life by, especially when you have a million options to choose from. Many pursue a purpose involving religion, spirituality, happiness, love, a hobby, friendship, family, or providing services. There is absolutely nothing wrong with living without an overall purpose or taking time to figure one or several out, so don't get discouraged. It is just helpful for some people. If you do have something you are passionate about, create reminders for yourself about it. Put up pictures, place stickers on your fridge, wear a button, get a tattoo, or sign up for news feeds to stimulate thoughts and

feelings regarding that passion no matter what mood you are in. You could even have a ritual with a group of people to commit to certain ideas and behaviors (Section 6.1). Doing so gives you a strong communal sense that even if life is difficult, you are going to maintain your commitments. Just remember that pursuing something simply for the sake of your personal happiness can hurt a lot of people; find sources of happiness that make many people happy rather than just yourself.

Succeeding creates happiness, but if you can be your genuine self while succeeding, you will also find a sense of meaning *(McGregor)*. You're not going to get a great emotional benefit out of succeeding in a job or relationship you find lackluster and limiting. This being the case, it is good to pursue hobbies and work you really enjoy and feel comfortable doing. What moves you?

9.15 - Spiritual, Religious, and Philosophical Pathways

A spiritual or religious pathway offers many healthy outlets for coping with depression and anxiety. Community, meditation, prayer, and meaning are just a few of the things that some spiritual and religious groups provide. These groups tend to be very supportive and a great way to make social connections as well.

While any belief system can be healthy, one must be careful with ideologies that preach mentally unhealthy ideas. One must also be careful of personally using spiritual, religious, and even philosophical beliefs as a means of justifying their depressive behaviors. I did this while growing up. The spiritual principles I created explained my symptoms of depression as something entirely else, and so I used my spirituality as an excuse to not seek help. This did act as a coping mechanism in its own way and assisted me in getting through my more troublesome years "safely," though I've witnessed others utilize spiritual principles in destructive acts either against themselves or others. I would not say that spirituality discovered through a depressed perspective negates those spiritual experiences, but I would deeply analyze what is an excuse for a depressive habit and what is truly spiritual or religious.

9.16 - Drop the Judgment

Judgment is the act of associating a thing with certain qualities, often without knowing those things to be true. Judgment is natural, and some judgments are important. We like some things and we dislike others, and speed up our decisions by applying experiences we've had before to similar experiences in the future. In a world with so much to judge though, judgments make us spend more time than we want thinking negatively, and in turn drive us into sadness, anger, and depression. Not only that, but judgments make communication and conflict resolution almost impossible, because they hide feelings and needs. "That is good" or "that is bad" statements give an individual very little information about how to proceed with a situation. This is especially the case when we dwell on our judgments and carry them around with us. Reworking judgments begins with becoming aware of them. The feelings created when we judge are almost instantaneous, so it is difficult to notice that the judgmental thoughts and the associated feelings are in fact separate. If you remove the judgments, the feelings will not arise. Judgment can be very subtle, such as when reading a book written in a way you dislike, or more overbearing, such as when you see someone dressed in a way you've always associated with something bad.

What do you lose by dropping your judgments of things or people? Probably nothing. What do you gain? A lot more happiness and opportunities to experience the world. Here are some tips for dropping judgment:

- Try for one day to not judge anyone; to genuinely live in the present moment without criticisms in order to give everyone a fair try.

- Check your ego. Everyone has something they are equally talented at as you are, and everyone has to start somewhere. Don't make assumptions about the capabilities of a person based on appearance or first impressions. Also note that everyone has their bad days, their sick days, their tired days, and their mournful days. Everyone also has had different opportunities and experiences in life to get to where they are now; sometimes difficulties and bad things happen along the way.

- Practice mindfulness meditation. Instead of thinking about your environment, fully experience the sensations created by that environment and your own body. This creates a state where there is no good or bad, there just is – there just is a phone ringing, there just is that particular person in the room, there just are cars honking, and there just is you in this space doing what you are doing with many objects around you.

- Judge and move on without holding onto the associated feelings.

- Judge and challenge yourself to do the opposite of what

your judgment tells you to do.

- When you experience anger toward a person, Marshal B. Rosenberg suggests to "replace the phrase 'I am angry because they...' with 'I am angry because I am needing'" *(Rosenberg 139)*. In this way you acknowledge your feelings to be the result of unmet needs you personally have rather than the actions of another person. The phrasing may help open a person up to meeting your needs rather than making them defensive when they feel judged. Of course this technique can be used for much more than the feelings of anger. See *Violent and Nonviolent Communication* (Section 10.4) for an overview of nonviolent communication.

9.17 - PTSD and Coming to Terms with a Traumatic Past

Some cases of depression are caused by events that occurred years ago. Confronting difficult experiences from the past can be liberating, and reduce stress. This is difficult, as traumatic events are often something people want to push out of their memory. However, they are another key to accepting oneself and understanding one's experience of depressed feelings and depression. Posttraumatic stress disorder (PTSD) impacts many people in minor to major ways. The process of confronting the inner demons causing negative responses can be a long one, but therapists will greatly help in the process. Ask your doctor for a therapist that specializes in PTSD treatment. If you'd like to start healing now, it may be helpful to fully separate from the causes of trauma and avoid situations that trigger traumatic memories. Doing so will provide a safe healing space and room for unraveling the reasons for your PTSD. Thoroughly understand your trauma and PTSD. Try writing about your past and emotions in detail and about how different events affect your current behavior and mood. A friend or family member may also give special insight into your memories if you are able to share your story openly. When you feel ready slowly reintroduce the traumatic triggers in a healthy environment. Either find acceptance with the triggers, or learn a new habit response to the habit cues such as deep breathing. Remember that this all takes time.

9.18 - Deal with the Negative Emotions You Have about Yourself and Others as Soon as Possible

Suffering is an important aspect of life. Growth and knowledge is found in these difficulties, and so it is generally good to work through it. In fact, avoiding dealing with negative emotions directed toward yourself or another person can quickly pull the whole mind into a state of depressed feelings or depression. Often the longer you wait to deal with these feelings, the harder the situation becomes to remediate and the worse the suffering becomes (granted that some time is necessary to process thoughts and react constructively to a situation). What do I mean by avoiding dealing with negative emotions? It is the lack of making a decision. Communicating with a friend, accepting certain qualities of a person, quitting a job, practicing mindfulness, or ending a relationship would all be potentially beneficial decisions, whereas complaining, venting, doing nothing, or obsessing over the negative qualities of a situation would constitute avoidance. Be proactive about your mental health.

As for altering negative feelings toward another person, there are two main ways. First, communicate to the person that you're upset with by using non-violent communication (see Section 10.4). State your feelings and observable facts in a neutral tone, but do not use name calling or slander. This may be easier after taking some space away from the source of your anger, but the sooner you deal with it the less it will consume you. If direct communication is difficult, a letter (or e-mail) may be used instead. A letter is helpful if you don't feel like you can remember everything you need to say, or even to just sort your thoughts out, but be aware that it is difficult to interpret a person's tone from letters. If a letter is used, it is best to directly hand it to the person and have them read it immediately so that any confusion can be clarified. This also avoids the anxiety created when waiting for a response.

If communication is not an option, or is too difficult, forgive the source of your suffering. Remember that everyone has their own difficulties, has their bad days, makes mistakes, and is constantly changing. Some personalities don't get along, but plenty more do. Why dwell on the negative when there are so many positive things to be experienced? Whenever your mind starts making a judgment or saying something hateful, say something nice, and focus on that instead. "He is such a jerk" could become "he is a very hard worker." Remind yourself that thinking hateful thoughts or making judgments is not helping anyone or teaching anyone a better method of being, and generally just hurts you. As mentioned in *Deep Breathing, Meditation, Mindfulness, Prayer, and Rituals* (Section 6.1) prayers of forgiveness may also help you let go of what has happened in the past. Since you cannot change what already happened, you may as well be content or happy with the idea that the universe meant it to happen for your personal story. Whether out of difficulty or happiness, regret gets you nowhere. Of course, you can learn from regret and act differently in the future, but right now, why dwell on the past?

9.19 - The Health of Stress, Sadness, and Anger

As you explore coping with depression and depressed feelings, you may attempt to avoid situations that create stress, sadness, anger, and other "negative" feelings. Know however that these are all parts of the human experience, and avoiding them is to avoid learning, growing, and even experiencing many positive aspects of life. As 2010 TEDxHouston speaker Brené Brown says, "vulnerability is kind of the core of shame and fear and our struggle for worthiness, but it appears that it is also the birthplace of joy, of creativity, of belonging, of love" *(Brown)*. When we try to numb an emotion, we numb the emotions we don't want to numb as well. Sometimes it is the negative or difficult experiences that make us find our happiness. Sometimes things just need to get really bad before you find the motivation to make changes in your life, or before you finally understand advice you heard years ago. Do your best to continue living your life, to communicate your needs and desires, and to take on an uncomfortable situation to get where you want to be. As I like to say, "hit rock bottom so hard you go straight through to the other side." In this way I do not ignore my suffering which has much to teach, but rather fully embrace it. Simultaneously these words help me keep in mind that I am trying to grow rather than become the same person I was before.

Uncomfortable situations provide a lot of motivation for creating constructive changes in our lives. Thus, seeing them as opportunities, rather than tragedies to be kept secret from ourselves, is very important to rediscovering a content and happy place. Welcome stress in as a challenge to grow from and overcome. As Rob Brezsny says, "engage in a relationship with the blind and sickly parts of yourself, perfect them, and you will awaken your hidden divinity" *(Brezsny 126)*. Of course, some suffering is just too much to digest quickly, and you may need to revisit it later once you have taken care of the immediate difficulties associated with that pain. I wish it were easier, and I wish that someone could provide some insight that would make it all go away or get it over with quicker, but in order to grow stronger, wiser, and happier, sometimes you need to figure out those hard experiences on your own. It is the trade-off we make for being human and living fulfilling lives.

10
Communication

10.1 - Communication Styles

How we communicate greatly impacts the way people treat us, and in turn plays a role in our relationships and moods. Communication is more than words and tone of voice, we also communicate through our clothing, activities, hair style, and body language. Part of a personality is displayed through these various factors, but it might be hard to realize how you are portraying yourself or what impact you are having on another person when you have communicated the way you do for so long. This is especially prevalent when interacting with different cultures. One culture may talk louder, and could be perceived as aggressive by others. Another culture may see themselves as polite, but be seen as passive or passive aggressive by others. City to city, state to state, coast to coast, and country to country there is a vast diversity of communication styles. Even within the same area, people grow up being better hands-on, auditory, or visual communicators. When people talk to us with a different style of communication, it may be difficult to know if that communication is emotionally charged or not. It is therefore important to consider cultural factors, not make assumptions, and have empathy when communicating. Asking questions is the key to understanding.

Sometimes our style of communication is not in line with how we want to be perceived nor used in a way that attracts the people we want in our lives. It takes a measure of mindfulness to determine why people treat you the way they do. You may have become complacent with this treatment and how new interactions don't always go so well, but perhaps you want to change that. Do you want to sound more confident, swear less, say positive things more often, stop using words like "umm" and "like," always have a joke handy as a conversation starter, or not be so argumentative? All of these are habits that take time to form or break. It may be helpful to practice alone to create new patterns of speech, and while in public note when you use a speech pattern you dislike.

10.2 - Introverts and Extroverts

There are distinctive social differences between introverts, extroverts, and shy people, and it is worth noting to yourself as well as your peers which trait(s) you tend toward. If you are not meeting your needs as an introvert or extrovert, it will increase your potential for depression. Susan Cain's New York Times bestseller, *Quiet*, describes the lesser understood introvert quite well. Debate exists over the exact definition of an introvert and extrovert, but the basic idea is that introverts need more alone time or quieter one-on-one social interaction to recharge their energy, whereas extroverts find social life and groups energizing *(Cain 12-14)*. Just because a person is introverted does not mean that they dislike groups or social interaction. Both introverts and extroverts can experience shyness, a trait describing social anxiety or hesitation toward strangers, acquaintances, and even friends. Unfortunately introverts are more likely to experience depression than extroverts due to a tendency of obsessively thinking over the same thought *(Law)*.

Everyone is on a spectrum between an introvert and extrovert, with few people fully taking on all the characteristics of one category. That said, the United States of America is dominated by extroverted thought in schools, work spaces, and culture, even though at least one third of the population consists of introverts *(Cain 3)*. If you are an introvert it is important to make your needs known. Not all these traits apply to everyone, and certainly no one is bound to them, but some characteristics associated with introverts include:

- Enjoyment of solitude or one-on-one interactions *(Cain 13-14)*.
- Dislike of small talk, risk-taking, and conflict.
- Better at listening than at talking.
- Works best alone and without interruption.
- Socially quieter than extroverts.
- Highly creative and thoughtful.
- Expresses oneself best through mediums such as writing or art instead of public speaking or group activities.
- Prefers friendly people over argumentative or conflict-oriented people *(Cain 231)*.
- Easily feels guilty *(Cain 234)*.
- Has trouble multitasking *(Cain 168)*.
- Has trouble accurately reading emotions and social cues during interactions with others *(Cain 236)*.

Introverts also tend to fit the category of "highly sensitive." According to Dr. Elaine Aron, people with high sensitivities often:

- Have strong observational skills.
- Avoid surprises.
- Experience exterior stimuli powerfully.
- Become anxious or underperform when others watch or

judge them.
- Notice emotional changes.
- Have strong empathetic feelings.
- Avoid unempathetic situations such as violent media.

(Cain 136-137)

Cain also asserts that introverts can temporarily thrive in extroverted environments, but eventually they need to find a "restorative niche." A restorative niche is where you can comfortably be yourself and recharge your energy, even for just a couple of minutes *(Cain 219)*. For an overwhelmed introvert these might include places like their room, nature, a quiet space with one other friend, or even a bathroom stall. Hopefully someday soon more people will acknowledge the needs of introverts and create an abundance of spaces that recharge rather than drain their energy, but until then establishing these places is likely up to you.

10.3 - Imaginary Conversations and Arguments

I find that any imaginary conversations or arguments in my head are unhealthy. Perhaps it can act as a rehearsal or way to vent out more extreme feelings for some, but it tends to make me feel worse or never talk to people I need to speak with. If you fall into this same pattern and catch yourself having conversations in your head, consider breathing deeply, writing out the conversation, or going directly to the person in question to speak with them.

10.4 - Violent and Nonviolent Communication

Our style of communication also impacts our ability to have needs met and deal with serious or argumentative conversations. According to Marshall B. Rosenberg, "violent" communication often incorporates:

- Moralistic judgments: "Value judgments reflect our beliefs of how life can best be served. We make moralistic judgments of people and behaviors that fail to support our value judgments" *(Rosenberg 17)*.
- Making comparisons: "[Dan Greenberg] suggests that if readers have a sincere desire to make life miserable for themselves, they might learn to compare themselves to other people" *(Rosenberg 18)*.
- Denial of responsibility: Expressing that something forces you to do or think a certain way. An example being "I started smoking because all my friends did," or "I cleaned my room because I had to" *(Rosenberg 19-20)*. In other words, it ignores why you personally took the action that you did. "I started smoking because I wanted to be closer with my friends," or "I cleaned my room because I wanted my friend to think I was a well-organized person" would be expressions taking responsibility for actions.
- Demand: A statement which threatens punishment if it is not completed *(Rosenberg 22)*.

These common methods of expressing needs and feelings are hostile and make ourselves or others defensive and closed off to the words spoken. They are also all "alienated expressions of our needs" *(Rosenberg 55)*. In other words, these hostile expressions can be reworded into unmet needs we personally have instead of attacks on a person. That is why Marshall B. Rosenberg created nonviolent communication, or NVC for short. NVC works by avoiding language that psychologically creates defensiveness and instead promotes language that creates openness. In his book, *Nonviolent Communication: A Language of Compassion*, he explains how to use observations, feelings, needs, and requests to navigate unmet needs you or others around you have *(Rosenberg 6)*.

Stating Unmet Needs You Have:

- Observe: What is it specifically that you like or don't like that a person is doing *(Nonviolent)*?
- State your feelings: How does the observed action make you feel? Does it make you feel happy, alive, afraid, bored, detached, angry, calm, etc.? Remember that a feeling is not a judgment; do not use slander or make accusations.
- State your needs. As mentioned in Section 9.1, common human needs include sustenance, safety, love, empathy, rest (recreation and play), community, creativity, autonomy (freedom), and meaning (purpose) What is your unmet need from the list above? Why do you personally want this change? How does it benefit you? Does it create more order, make work go faster, create a quieter space, make a higher quality product, etc.? Needs explain your feelings.
- Make a request: Make it clear, polite, reasonable, and preferably a "do" instead of a "don't." Remember, you are making a request, not a demand. "Could you please rewrite this with more action language," or, "can you start thinning the carrots to quarter-foot spaces?"
- Example: "James, when you play your electric guitar past 10:00 PM (observation), I feel frustrated (feeling) because I need to wake up for work early (need). Could you keep your playing to before 10:00PM (request)?

Stating Unmet Needs Others Have:

- Observe and listen: What is the person expressing they like or dislike?
- Clarifying question: Make sure the person knows you

understand what they like or dislike and the reason why. You may not agree with them, but it is important that a person feels that you are listening and can empathize with them. For instance, "are you anxious because you are needing a quieter space," or, "so you feel angry because some stranger yelled at you?"

- State your feelings and needs or ask to offer advice, but do this only once the other person feels adequately heard.

Non-Judgmental Language

The key with phrasing is to use non-judgmental language. Many words we use to describe feelings are actually evaluations of the other person, or how we interpret their actions *(Rosenberg 44)*. This includes words such as "attacked, cheated, manipulated, provoked, rejected," and "unwanted *(Rosenberg 44)*." Work on removing judgmental language from your vocabulary. Instead of jumping to conclusions, consider the many reasons for a person acting the way that they did, or better yet, try to connect with a person by asking them about their needs. "Are you feeling angry because _____?" When asking these questions, do not blame yourself by using "I." Try to guess their unmet needs that are at the root of their suffering. See *Drop The Judgment* (Section 9.16) for more information.

Suggestions

- Keep it short and simple so it is easier for people to listen.
- Ask people to "do" instead of "not do."
- All components of the non-violent communication model (observation, feelings, needs, requests) are needed or the interaction can quickly become either violent or misunderstood. However, words may be rephrased to sound more natural. For instance the example with James and the

electric guitar could be phrased, "James, when you play your electric guitar past 10:00PM (observation), I become frustrated (feeling) because I wake up for work early (need). Could you keep your playing to before 10:00PM (request)?"

- Think about what you're going to say before you say it, or even write it out beforehand.
- Never make an assumption about why a person does something. Only speak from observable facts and clarify the truth by asking questions.
- To practice NVC go back to conversations that haven't gone so well in the past and rewrite them using non-violent communication.

NVC is a complicated technique and involves even more than the basics covered here. For more NVC guidance, read the book, watch video tutorials, and seek out local workshops. It's not something I would say for any other material, but *Nonviolent Communication: A Language of Compassion* should be part of all formal education, or even required reading for the human race. It's a powerful and life changing tool!

11
Depression Related to Life Experiences

The story of our mental health begins before birth, starting from the actions of our parents. It continues with our biological sex, upbringing, socioeconomic status, culture, and the discrimination we experience as a result of our culture and other cultures.

11.1 - Hormones

All people experience hormonal fluctuations regardless of their biological sex. These fluctuations in hormones, especially testosterone and estrogen, regulate many things and can heavily influence mood, though the science is not yet well understood. Males and females both have testosterone and estrogen, but males generally have more testosterone and females more estrogen. If you have never experienced severe depression until your 30s, 40s, or 50s, or if your depressive episodes occur cyclically on a daily or monthly basis, you may have hormonal depression. Talk to your doctor about having your hormone levels tested and possibly seeking hormone therapy. You may be instructed to consume or not consume certain foods high in estrogen or testosterone, or you may be prescribed treatment which boosts your hormone levels.

Testosterone

In a survey of studies, low, or very high levels of testosterone were found to create depressive episodes in males (*Johnson JM*). High testosterone is also associated with confidence, aggression, and sex drive. Testosterone levels fluctuate throughout a male's day, month, year, and lifetime (*Diamond*). On a given day, testosterone levels are highest in the morning and lowest before going to sleep, so depressive episodes may be more likely for males in the evening.

Estrogen, Premenstrual Syndrome (PMS), Premenstrual Dysphoric Disorder (PMDD), and Postpartum Depression

Estrogen also cycles daily, monthly, and over a female's lifetime (*Bao*). The hormone regulates serotonin levels, with higher levels associated with a reduction in stress (*Amin; Beck*). That said, there is no direct correlation between low estrogen levels and mood (*Todd*). Low levels of estrogen, however, may increase the potential of experiencing depression under specific circumstances (*Lokuge)*. For instance, estrogen may interact with other hormones and chemicals to cause depressive moods during menstrual cycles, pregnancy, giving birth to a child, and aging.

About once a month many females experience premenstrual syndrome (PMS), which causes light to severe physical and mental symptoms such as cramps and mood swings. One in five females experience mild depression each cycle and one in twenty experience more severe symptoms with debilitating depression *(Pearlstein)*. Premenstrual dysphoric disorder (PMDD) is described as a severe form of premenstrual syndrome. However, there is debate about whether PMDD is a real condition or just a combination of others *(Daw)*. While cyclical, PMDD may proliferate through an already stressed or depressed mind. Most of the common coping techniques such as eating well, sleeping right, relaxing, and exercising can help relieve symptoms of PMS and PMDD. The following can also help:

- Taking L. Tryptophan, an amino acid, from "the time of ovulation to the third day of menstruation" *(S. Steinberg)*.
- Taking vitamin B-6 *(Wyatt)*.
- Taking the herb Vitex agnus -castus, or chaste tree, can help, but interacts with other medicines *(Vitex)*.
- Supplementing with calcium carbonate, magnesium, and vitamin E helps relieve symptoms of PMS and thus may also help with PMDD *(Bhatia)*.
- Quitting smoking (*Vann*).
- Not consuming caffeine or alcohol during PMS (*Vann*).
- Taking oral contraceptives (*Vann*).
- Accepting your symptoms of PMS as a natural and positive part of your life and personality (*Grish*). Speaking to a therapist may help.
- Several pharmaceutical antidepressant SSRIs have been effective at treating PMDD *(S. Meir)*. Talk with your doctor.

Hormonal fluctuations during pregnancy and after giving birth also causes many mothers to experience postpartum depression. While no scientific research has been completed regarding it, some believe that consuming the placenta (placentophagy) after giving birth will help prevent this type of depression, as well as having a number of other benefits *(Donovan)*. In this method the placenta is dried and put into capsules to be eaten over a period of time. The theory is that because most other animals perform placentophagy, humans should too, and that the act balances hormones. Postpartum depression can also be dealt with by using coping mechanisms outlined throughout this guide.

11.2 - Pregnancy

If pregnant, check with your doctor before taking any medications or herbal supplements. Some medication usage just requires closer monitoring by a medical professional, but others, like most antidepressants, should not be taken at all. In the latter case, you'll have to seek alternatives to pharmaceuticals to deal with your depression.

11.3 - Depression in Children

A child's mental health begins before birth, in the womb (*Ryrie 23*). Mothers who eat a proper diet are much more likely to give birth on time and to a baby with a healthy weight, two factors linked to youth happiness and better cognitive ability later in life. Children raised on breast milk receive an important balance of essential fatty acids linked to proper brain development. Keep in mind that anything consumed, including medicines, will be present in your breast milk, and some of these things are not healthy for babies.

The season a child is born in influences their mental health as well (*European*). In one study of 400 participants, summer children were found to have greater mood swings, but along with spring children, were happier. People born in the winter time were less irritable, but more depressed. Fall children experienced less depression than those born in the winter.

Once born, a healthy diet for your child is essential in maintaining their mood and behavior. See *Food* (Section 7.1) for general information on a healthy diet. Children and pregnant persons do have different nutritional requirements than others, so if possible, you should do your research before caring for a child or becoming pregnant! See a prenatal fact sheet online for more information.

Most importantly, a mentally healthy child comes from mentally healthy parents and a stable community. Ensure you are taking care of yourself, your child's emotional and social needs are being met, and you have a supportive community to help you through the process.

11.4 - Depression in Teenagers

As a teenager, you may have little control over the causes feeding your depression. This is because of oppression by factors that cannot easily be changed. Examples include family, age, where you live, and discrimination. Huge neurological and hormonal changes are also happening that can be very confusing in a culture that does not often talk about them. Having been through it myself, I want to apologize for the awful support teenagers receive to escape unhealthy and traumatizing environments, and want to assure you that it will get better. Outlets exist, they just aren't always taught to teenagers. These include getting a GED to finish high school early, dual enrolling in a community college, transferring schools or transferring to an "alternative school," seeking legal emancipation from your family, talking to parents about seeing a therapist or having family therapy, talking to a counselor, attending summer camps, or applying for travel or exchange programs. Making art and music or experiencing it is a great outlet as well. You might also consider sharing your difficulties with friends at school or online.

11.5 - Depression in Older Adults

Old age is a time to celebrate and live fully. There are places to go, stories to tell, and people to keep in touch with. That said, growing older also comes with many trials. These include hormonal changes, physical changes, weakening of the body, a greater risk of life-threatening diseases, seeing loved ones pass away, and being confronted with death. Much of the material already covered in this book will help with these transitions, especially maintaining a healthy lifestyle with exercise, wholesome food, and a strong community of friends and family. The writings of Thich Nhat Hanh and other Buddhist teachers offer meditations and discourses on finding acceptance with death as well. It takes time to make these transitions, but you can find great joy and fulfillment in your later years.

11.6 - Poverty, Riches, and Jobs

Growing up poor increases the potential of experiencing depression *(Kim)*. Not only that, but one study correlates higher income to an increase in emotional well-being and "life evaluation," or the "thoughts that people have about their life when they think about it" *(Kahneman)*. People who are richer and more educated evaluate their life as better, and household earnings up to $75,000 (U.S. average in 2010) correlate to improved emotional well-being.

Money can bring a lot of comfort to life, but so can a fulfilling job and healthy work environment. Many people lose themselves in money to the point of disliking their work and having no life outside of increasing their earnings. Find work that you can balance with an active and social life. If you don't earn as much as you'd like to, consider going back to school. Journeyman positions and two year technical degrees are a good place to look if paying for college is daunting. Internships and volunteer positions provide new job experiences and help open new job horizons too. Whatever you do, just be more than those dollar bills.

11.7 - Cultural Upbringing

Factors such as where you were born and raised, what culture your parents come from, and where you have been living impacts your emotional well-being. For instance, cultural aspects of the United States of America that might impact your mental health include:

- An emphasis on individuality over community.
- Paid vacation and maternity leave is limited.
- Minimum wage is not a living wage.
- Consuming unhealthy food is portrayed as cool and socially acceptable.
- An eclectic mix of religious, scientific, and spiritual beliefs.
- A political system dominated by only two parties.
- Beauty standards set by magazines and television shows are impossible to obtain or inaccessible to the majority of body types.
- Preventative medicine is usually unsupported by medical professionals and health insurance companies.
- Sources of environmental degradation and pollution go unchecked by government officials until citizens unite and petition for something to be done.
- Access to media is always available.

The political atmosphere, gender norms, medical systems, labels, holidays, traditions, history, ideas of what constitutes depression, communication styles, sleeping patterns, birthing practices, marriage rituals, words, religions, foods, etc. of an area all play into who you are as an individual, how you relate to your surroundings, and impact your potential to experience depression. When everyone around you does something, and you have been raised to do that thing yourself, seeing how it impacts your emotions can be difficult. Be culturally literate by studying other cultures and understanding how your culture relates to others. Also ask yourself what learned behaviors influence your social and emotional world. By doing so you can begin seeing what is mentally healthy or unhealthy as a whole culture and seek solutions. Consider participating in volunteer, activist, and advocacy groups (see Chapter 12) to help change your culture into a more mentally healthy one.

11.8 - If You Experience Depression Associated with Discrimination

Depression arises from experiencing oppression related to gender, race, body image, culture, income level, age, and ability discrimination. Discrimination is deeply rooted in the United States of America and elsewhere, and while conditions might be improving for some groups, there is still a lot of work to be done before everyone feels safe and respected. People who experience oppression may also have a harder time accessing the techniques outlined throughout this guide because of time, money, or community restraints. However, if you can:

- Form a caucus or peer group of people you identify with and with whom you can safely talk about the discrimination you experience and what can be done about it in your local community. Also connect with people online.
- Relocate to a place with more people you identify with or away from oppressive people.
- Remind people of their privileges and call them out (or preferably "in") on their oppressive behaviors, or get allies to do so for you. Preferably, calling people out is done with the techniques outlined by nonviolent communication. See

Violent and Nonviolent Communication (Section 10.4) and *Advocacy, Volunteering, and Activism* (Chapter 12) for more information.

- Do your best to focus on the positive and live in the present moment. It's not good for you to dwell on things out of your control, but it can be helpful to channel negative feelings created from discrimination into fighting oppression, exercising, making art, or other constructive outlets.

- Seek out help from a therapist knowledgeable about the type of discrimination that you experience. Be sure that you feel comfortable with them and that their politics resonate with yours. Switch therapists if you feel threatened or judged. Every therapist is different, so you may need to try several out before finding the right one. Read more about therapy in Section 9.5.

12
Advocacy, Volunteering, and Activism

Being an activist[A], or a person trying to create broader change in the world, is a fulfilling role to take on. Attempting to

---

A   The words activist, advocate, and volunteer are used interchangeably.

make society and the world into a better place brings a great amount of meaning to one's life. However, it can also be very difficult and often means dealing with guilt, anger, cultural deprivation, as well as anxiety while attempting to create change against enormous resistance. Considering the negative remarks received externally and internally to the group, a person must be careful with their mental wellness while engaged in activist struggles. Sometimes the culture surrounding activist groups, and activism in general, is simply not mentally healthy. Even if the work done is good for other people or the planet, it can still hurt individuals. The following suggestions and observations are therefore meant to make you aware of how these influences can trigger depression or depressed feelings and lead to burnout. With this knowledge it is up to you to change the culture surrounding your activism, to step back from it, or balance it with other mentally healthy activities. More than anything, just remember that you are important too and that a content and happy mind is much more effective at creating positive change.

This chapter was the most difficult to write in the whole guide. It's a complicated subject area and just like everything else there are suggestions that may not be for everyone. Please do not be offended if something here does not fit your personal ideas, for some it can be useful. There is a lot of mental health discrimination based on one's ability to perform a task (ableism) within the advocacy, volunteer, and activism fields. Be sure to check yourself before making accusations or putting too much work on any one person, including yourself.

12.1 Prepare Yourself

Many people jump into causes they have very little knowledge of, and try to create change without the right tools. Doing the following things will make you much more effective and lessen your frustration!

- Research both sides of an argument and try to walk in the shoes of the opposing belief.
- Study some human psychology and sociology–look into how to effectively communicate, what makes a good flyer, what basic human needs are, and what successful activist campaigns have done in the past.
- Look at examples of effective propaganda throughout history.
- Know how much time you are going to devote to being an activist and how much time you are going to reserve for self-care.
- Have a supportive community that does not involve your campaign work, or at least does not always talk about it. Your life is more than just work and intense conversations!

12.2 - Balance Time

The most important thing to consider during times of difficulty in an advocacy, volunteer, or activist group is that even the smallest accomplishment is moving towards positive results. Changing the status quo takes time, so remind yourself that success is possible by watching or reading about previous campaigns, or by speaking to older peers within your movement. Also consider the amount of work you personally take on to reach a given goal. Are you doing more than you can handle? It's easy to believe that everything will collapse if you reduce the amount of work you do, but the more long-term work you can do, the better. Why not take actions that are more manageable, or recruit new members? Working on small goals that show immediate results provides mental rewards that boost personal and group wellness. Ensuring needs are met to create a group of well-rested and positive people may also make it easier to recruit new members.

It is important to realize that as an activist, one is not living the life they would be living if the world fit their desires. What would you be doing otherwise? I believe it is important to occasionally live that life, or incorporate parts of it into your life. It's also okay to stop and take a rest if things get too stressful. Know your limitations and establish them with your peers. Pass the work on when you reach that limit, because it is better to say "no" to new tasks than it is to become overwhelmed, ignore your personal health, and never return to the group. For balancing time, only intake news media that is related to what you are working with or directly impacting you locally so as not to drown in negativity. Sure, all world events are important, but if you cannot or are choosing not to do anything about them, then you are needlessly pushing your mind into negative spaces. Use this time instead for cultivating positivity and contentment.

12.3 - Cultural Deprivation and Creating an Alternative Culture

Some activists reject mainstream culture and do their best to create what they can of an alternative culture. With only a limited number of people to celebrate this culture though, it can be difficult to maintain and lead to cultural deprivation. However, I believe that a solid culture is essential for a healthy mind and healthy community. Create a community identity with boundaries and traditions. Boundaries state how your community functions and what the allowable limits are. They might include things like how to speak, meeting procedures, substance policies, and membership termination rules. Traditions provide a reason for people to gather and celebrate the important events time has unveiled in their lives and cultural history. They act as reminders of historical events and give emphasis to what it means to be part of a collective identity. Traditions can also help bring attention to your cause for outsiders to plug into, for instance, an annual parade, benefit party, or story-sharing circle. Continue to celebrate, even if you have to make up your own holidays or traditions! It is also okay to continue to celebrate mainstream holidays, just do so as responsibly as possible and add your own flair to them.

12.4 - Communication

If you are an activist, advocate, or volunteer (or even if you aren't), please stop whatever you're doing right now and go read *Nonviolent Communication: A Language for Compassion* by Marshall B. Rosenberg. If you can, read it to your peers as well. Many of us were never taught how to communicate, but just pieced together what we could from growing up in our communities and the media we ingested. NVC teaches how to communicate with basic human needs in mind. I believe it is a very powerful tool for reaching personal fulfillment, creating smoother group dynamics, and advancing group goals. It was developed specifically for helping people verbally mediate through their problems instead of killing each other in areas with a lot of racial violence. Now it is used in communities, with couples, between different cultures, in wars, and in conflict situations in general. While perhaps not always the right method, I believe it is a very useful tool for activists to become more effective and happier with their work and in their respective communities or groups. You can read an overview of Rosenberg's book in *Violent and Nonviolent Communication* (Section 10.4). I emphasize the reading of this book for activists because of the amount of aggressive and judgmental communication I have experienced activist groups use and in turn alienate people from important causes. In fact, one study titled "The ironic impact of activists: Negative stereotypes reduce social change influence" found that people did not support environmentalist and feminist causes due to what they saw as "eccentric and militant" behavior *(Bashir)*. A person will generally believe in your cause, it's just that they need your cause presented in a way that respects their culture, beliefs, and character. This has implications in both your verbal communication and your non-verbal communication such as body language and clothing. Naturally, NVC is not always possible, or the right option, but it is a useful method in many situations.

When you are attacked by someone, responding with violent communication may sometimes be beneficial. While violent communication is not ideal, remaining silent to injustices creates no change. Responding violently may be your only option when there is little time between standing up for yourself and never seeing a person again. A violent rebuttal more than anything gives your ego a boost (though can also make you feel worse), and may also make a definitive awareness that the thing said was problematic. However this is very dependent upon how the perpetrator communicates and thinks. Violent communication mostly works by silencing wrongdoers. It does not necessarily alter their perception of groups of people. In fact, violent communication may reinforce negative feelings toward groups of people, so use it sparingly. That is why I highly suggest learning nonviolent communication, because it tries to create openness and dialogues to reach understanding between people. It also forces you to slow down and think about how you are speaking before possibly making a violent situation even more violent.

There has been some backlash against using nonviolent communication, but from what I have collected, this antagonism stems from people who have experienced the improper usage of NVC. Or rather, something that sounds like NVC but is not NVC at all. From speaking with people about this backlash, it seems that their understanding of NVC is primarily from personal interactions or workshops, rather than directly from the work of Marshall B. Rosenberg. NVC is a fairly complicated tool and takes time to master. A one or two hour workshop does not cover the breadth of content Rosenberg covers in his book, video, and audio tutorials. In turn we have a massive body of people who use the basics of NVC but are unaware of aspects of it beyond that. I believe a synthesis of all methods of learning NVC must be used to have a thorough understanding of the technique. Another aspect of the backlash against nonviolent communication is that people experience it being used to manipulate others. However, NVC is a tool, and just like any tool, it has its time and place, and can be used for "good" or for "bad." To refuse to use NVC just because of how others have used it is rather silly.

Here are some general suggestions for communicating as an activist:

- Try your best to call people in, not out. Or in other words, have a conversation with people instead of communicating aggressively. Yelling, seeking revenge, or speaking hatefully, rarely, if ever, convinces a person that they are wrong. These forms of violent communication tend to worsen the mood of both parties and breed thoughts of revenge and feelings of anger.

- A person who enters into an argument with you or makes statements with anger or violence often must first be mediated with to listen to your side. Your goal is to calm them down by openly listening to their needs without reacting in argument, criticism, or judgment. Ask questions. You can state your side once they have calmed down and moved from the emotional to rational side of thought.

- Have empathy, remembering that everyone has basic needs to fulfill, troubles to take care of, and come from a past you know nothing or very little about.

- Use positive reinforcement. Positive reinforcement is more effective than negative reinforcement (such as yelling) because rewarding a person for good behavior gives them a reason to exhibit a new behavior, whereas punishing someone for a bad behavior does nothing toward showing them an alternative.

- Those who ignore or mock your desire for change may not be willing to alter their behaviors. It may be best to not waste your time on these individuals.

Other materials that have helped activist groups transform into more positive and effective bodies of change include *Communicating Across The Divides In Our Everyday Lives*, *The Work That Reconnects* <www.joannamacy.net> and *The Three Principles* <www.centerforsustainablechange.org>. Don Schneider's book, *Communicating Across The Divides In Our Everyday Lives*, is a "psychological field manual for constructive dialogue about social and environmental concerns and the progress of civilization" (Schneider). It talks about different character styles that people communicate through and how to create meaningful conversations with people who disagree with your world views. *The Work That Reconnects* is a spiritual methodology aiming to "[help] us discover our innate connections with each other and with the self-healing powers in the web of life" *(Macy)*. According to Joanna Macy, the author, "this aim is essential for the emergence of a life-sustaining culture." *The Three Principles* are Mind, Consciousness, and Thought *(Principles)*. According to the Center for Sustainable Change, "when people realize they create their own mental suffering via the Principles, they begin to realize the resilience, wisdom, beauty and genuine potential for a gratifying life that lies within them—beyond their limited, personal thoughts."

12.5 Privilege and Guilt

Many activists also experience guilt regarding their lifestyle or position of privilege, especially from the blame they receive from other activists.

- If you are called out as oppressive by someone, it is okay. Apologize, listen, and try to ask questions if it is not apparent why the thing said was offensive. Do your own research to become informed on the type of oppression. Acknowledge that there is deeply rooted discrimination and oppression in the United States of America and elsewhere, and that while you may not mean to offend anyone, you grew up in a culture that oppresses others. As such, also keep in mind that it is not so much you being called out as is the culture of oppression, which includes things like racism, sexism, classism, ableism, and ageism.

- Who you are and what you're doing is okay, even if that means indulging in mainstream culture or your personal privileges. Even the smallest contributions to "positive" change are still a lot more than what most people provide. In fact, no matter how you go about it, partaking in industrialized civilization directly or indirectly oppresses a human being or other living entity. Even so, working within systems of oppression generally allows you to create much more positive change than if you separated yourself from civilization and were "completely" anti-oppressive. No one is perfect, and that is okay. Be grateful for the privileges you were born with and do your best to use them constructively, but only do what you can within the limits of your mental health and personal wellness. Oppression is fought much better with a positive mindset!

- Just because someone says something is "bad" does not necessarily mean it is, so do your own research. Become informed and do not jump onto bandwagons of new ideas. Many activist, volunteer, and advocacy groups practice forms of globalization and imperialism and are insensitive to the differences between cultures worldwide.

- What one person, group, or culture thinks is offensive or oppressive changes depending on the person, group, or culture being interacted with. Do your best not to be oppressive or offensive, but realize that you will need to change your language and actions depending on who you are around. That is why asking questions and not making assumptions is so important while interacting with others. Note that it is impossible and unhealthy to attempt to please everyone at all times. You can only do the best that you can do and sometimes that means learning through mistakes.

- Watch out for working with people who practice oppressive anti-oppression (see next section).

12.6- Blame and Oppressive Anti-Oppression

Other activists live with a lot of blame and hatred of the lifestyles and privileges of others. People who spread the teachings of anti-oppression with these feelings sometimes fall into oppressive behaviors themselves. This group is one of the greatest internal challenges activists face today because while well-meaning, they often make activist circles into alienating, offensive, exclusive, ineffective, negative, or triggering spaces. They should be mediated with or removed from the group to help maintain mental wellness, effectiveness, and positivity. Teaching nonviolent communication to these individuals is one remediation process. Doing so will give them a broader understanding of how communication impacts people and an alternative to how they speak.

Below are the traits of oppressive anti-oppresors. Some of the listed items are important to use or completely reasonable in certain instances, but the line can generally be drawn between someone who is experiencing discrimination or oppression first-hand and someone who is reacting to it as an ally[A]. Even with this line, many of the traits are not constructive and will not make the world into a less oppressive space. Of course, persons who are the target of oppressive behaviors have every right to react how they please. Allies, however, should be especially careful with how they inform others because they are speaking for another person or group of people. The following are associated with oppressive anti-oppression:

- Poor communication through aggressive speaking, slander, refusing to mediate with an individual, using technical "radical" or activist terms without defining them, or passive-aggressiveness[B].
- Over-emphasis on attacking or ostracizing individuals rather than the institutions which perpetuate oppression. Of course working on oppression at the individual and institutional levels are both important, but much greater change is created by reforming institutions that create oppressive individuals. Existing institutions must be altered or new institutions created for large changes to take place.
- Categorizing ignorance as oppressive, even if a person is open-minded and has grown up in a culture devoid of anti-oppressive ideologies. That, or forgetting that "radical" or "alternative" ideas take time to form, and people who are

A   An 'ally' is a person who fights against a type of discrimination they do not personally experience.

B   Passive-aggressiveness is a behavior in which a person is not forward about their negative feelings and display them indirectly through things such as silence, glares, or generalized anger unrelated to the reasons for which they are actually angry. This is very common on the West Coast of the USA.

"aware" generally go through specific experiences to reject "mainstream" ideologies. Generally this is paired with passive-aggressive speaking so that the person never actually becomes aware of their oppressive act, or is spoken to in such a way that they are not allowed to be open-minded. It is also problematic in recruitment situations where people who are more aware of oppression and their personal privileges deny membership to a person who may be open-minded but has never been exposed to ideas outside of mainstream culture. This is especially hypocritical when the recruiters were once just as ignorant; everyone needs to start somewhere.

- Ignoring personal privileges or acts of oppression while calling someone else out on their privileges. No one is perfect, and everyone is an oppressor on some level. We can only work toward becoming less oppressive and safer individuals by practicing peaceful, direct, and nonviolent communication while following principles of sustainability and changing the institutions which perpetuate the oppression of all life forms.
- Forcing ideas of right or wrong onto another culture and perpetuating globalization and the destruction of culture.
- Mocking religious or spiritual practices and in turn creating unsafe spaces for practitioners of different beliefs.
- Assuming the privileges of another person. Without first asking it is impossible to know what a person's ethnicity, gender, sex, mental conditions, or life background is.
- Calling people out but not in. Criticizing but never showing gratitude.
- Emphasizing human oppression but ignoring environmental oppression, or emphasizing environmental oppression but ignoring human oppression.
- Ignoring psychological and cultural differences between

many peoples and assuming all actions or mentalities are a personal choice. Examples creating psychological differences include brain chemistry altered from heavy metal poisoning, premature birth, or various childhood experiences. Cultural differences include places a person was born and how they were raised and taught to communicate.

12.7 - Substance Abuse

The stresses that activists experience lead some to use substances as coping mechanisms to fight depression or stop thoughts and feelings. Substances such as alcohol and tobacco often make depression worse, however. This substance abuse can be difficult to avoid in alternative or activist social circles. It may be worthwhile to have a discussion regarding it among your peers—why do you use substances? What role does it play? Is it a coping mechanism? What does it say regarding the time you are giving for your personal health? Consider creating alternative social venues and positive coping mechanisms, such as a running club or a collaborative art group. See *What Substances to Avoid* (Section 7.3) for more information, including support groups for narcotics and alcohol.

12.8 - Policies

Certain policies greatly minimize negative feelings in activist groups. Consider having these easily accessible or posted in your meeting place. For instance:

- Have a membership termination policy that is fair, easily enacted, and that people feel comfortable using. At some point someone who brings down the mood of everyone will come on board and impede your purpose.

- Create a new member orientation that hypes up and educates the new members. Support new members speaking up about problems in a constructive manner.

- Look at different meeting and voting models and choose one that best suits your purpose. People often get bogged down with meetings, so find ways to make them fun and streamlined. Having a check-in question, games, and a person who has taken facilitation classes are very helpful. Also decide on methods of calming an emotional meeting or knowing when to table an agenda item.

12.9 - Breaking Away from "Us" versus "Them"

Many activists have a perspective of "us" versus "them," but this is not healthy because it tends to dehumanize the "other" side and creates negative assumptions and generalizations about "them." These mental formations make "us" see "them" as all the same, even though a group of people have a diversity of personalities and almost certainly are not all the same. When "them" is collectively denounced as doing something "bad," "us" also has a harder time connecting with "them" on an empathetic level because "us" has the expectation that a person from "them" is a wrongdoer and not capable of becoming an ally. Since labeling a whole group with judgments is inherently a violent form of communication, "us" increases the likelihood that either side will respond to one another with more violent forms of communication. In turn "them" becomes more resistant to change.

Most everyone is just trying to get by and actually has the same basic needs, no matter what their upbringing is (see a list of basic human needs in Section 9.1). Relating your vision of the world to those basic needs is one of the most powerful ways of speaking to any culture or sort of person. Instead of generalizing a group of people (women, men, trans people, whites, blacks, Native Americans, Hispanics, people from the United States of America, socialists, communists, capitalists, hipsters, bros, etc), speak one-on-one with individuals who do not meet your personal needs with nonviolent communication (see Section 10.4). Challenge yourself to have empathy before you express anger, and think about what unmet needs you and the person you are communicating with have before speaking. Most of all, avoid creating stereotypes for groups. It only alienates people from one another and reinforces those behaviors!

The concept of "good" and "bad" changes from culture to culture and is actually an expression of needs *(Rosenberg 54)*. When "us" says something "them" does is "bad," "us" is essentially saying "them" are bad for doing this thing. Underlying the accusation is an unmet need "us" personally has. When this unmet need is in the form of a judgmental statement it tends to weaken or break down communication. Speaking from personal needs and feelings rather than only stating the values of a group or culture allows people to listen and understand each other much better. For instance, saying "killing is wrong" versus "when people are killed in the war I feel upset because I want everyone to be able to live a life free of violence." Do you see the difference? In one a judgment is made, while in the other the person states their specific feelings and needs surrounding their value that killing is wrong. Speaking in this manner, "us," opens the doorway to being treated with compassion and empathy, and in turn listened to. In other words, try to explain your feelings and needs instead of generalizing things as "good" or "bad."

"Us" versus "them" mentalities also foster the idea that one is out to destroy something. Why not first create something that will benefit "us" and can potentially be enjoyed by "them" as well? It feels much better, establishes more allies, and without an alternative for people to go to, what is destroyed will almost certainly come back.

12.10 - Make It Fun

Finally, make activism fun. Be sure that you are including humor, silliness, and social downtime with your work. Positivity and love are the most powerful tools activists can use to fight for their causes. They not only help draw new people in but also prevent burnout for existing members. Consider celebrating the things that are important to you, playing games, or making your informational materials especially artful and full of humor. With meetings, start off with a silly check-in question and game. Bring the community together with child-friendly potlucks and educational games. Most activist groups are small enough that you have a lot of power to enact change, so do your best to alter the mundane status quo.

13
Managing a Depressive Episode

13.1 - If You Have a Depressive Episode

Read the list of triggers in Chapter 4 to help figure out what the cause of your depression is. Focus on addressing that trigger if possible and communicating with any necessary parties. Here are some other options depending on how you feel:

- Remove yourself from overstimulating environments.
- Create a safe environment by cleaning your room, putting on music, etc.
- Seek out help from someone such as a friend, therapist, or doctor. Everything is easier with reassurance and support from others.
- Write. Process the thoughts in your head, recall the best moments of your life, or figure out where you want to be and how to get there.

- Meditate and practice mindfulness. Don't allow repetitive negative thoughts to take over. Find contentment and goodness in the present moment.
- Trust that what your brain says is untrue and disconnected from your rationality. Trust that the feelings will pass if you take care of yourself.
- Go to sleep.
- Play a game, read a book, or watch something that will occupy your mental energy.
- Admit yourself into a psychiatric ward and put yourself into the full care of medical professionals until you get better.
- Call a support line like the National Suicide Hotline at 1-800-273-8255.

13.2 - If You Have a Depressive Episode Associated with a Negative Occurrence

If you have a depressive episode caused by external factors such as the death of a loved one or breaking up with your partner, there are a number of ways to cope with it. First realize that only time can heal some emotional injuries. The eventual goal is to keep living fully with activities, friends, and things that help maintain stability in your life. Until then have a safe space, whether it be a person or place, where you feel comfortable and unthreatened. See, call, or write a friend or family member to whom you can relate the experience. Hopefully they can reassure you and help calm some of your feelings. If explaining your situation is difficult, more subtly ask for a hug or just to hang out and do something like watching a movie. This may be an easier means of understanding you are indeed loved and provide some calming energy. Another option is to use a non-destructive act that pulls your mind away from obsessive negative thoughts. These acts might include reading a book, working on art, socializing, going to sleep on time, meditating, watching television, listening to music, exercising, playing a game, or other methods outlined in this guide.

Sometimes bad feelings over an event won't go away until you genuinely want them to. Saying "this is the first day of my life" or "it is silly that I'm still feeling like this, I'm moving on" can break you free of feelings you are holding onto. Other times feeling really awful will inspire you to create a new life. And yet other times you just need to wait until you run into the right person, make a new friend, or communicate to certain people about your grievances. Whatever you do though, try your best to keep pursuing your hobbies and social life—it will increase the likelihood of being knocked back onto stable ground.

13.3 - If Someone You Care about Has a Depressive Episode

Inevitably a friend, family member, or peer will become depressed. They may seem unfamiliar and act in a manner that is difficult for you. This is because their sense of reality has changed. If you choose to help, you will need to discuss their thoughts with them while dispelling false ones, as well as figuring out the root cause of their depression. It is difficult to help someone who doesn't want to be helped, but if they do, the end goal is to de-escalate extreme emotions, resume thinking within terms of their normal reality, and help them realize how to prevent a similar episode in the future. Generally a few ideas to follow while helping a person are:

- Don't tell a person that they have a condition.
- Don't tell a person that "what you're saying is not true."
- Don't treat a person as inferior.
- Not all truths need to be spoken.

- Do let a person know that you are there for them and that their presence makes you happy.
- Do empathize with a person's feelings and show that you hear them.
- Do ask to give advice before giving advice.
- Do allow a person to experience their pain constructively.

The best thing you can do for a person is just be there for them; hang out and get them to continue socializing and experiencing new things with you. Beyond that, you'll need to analyze several items and respond accordingly. First, do they know they are depressed? At times it can be very difficult for a person to acknowledge that their behavior and mood are out of the ordinary. Some people you know may have even been depressed for many years of their life and it is now their norm. Try starting a conversation with them about it. "You've seemed sort of down recently, is anything the matter?" If their depression is longer standing, you might bring up an instance that you believe changed their mental state, or some memory that they dwell upon, and help them work through it. Stay away from bringing up traumatic memories though! If they don't acknowledge their depression, try incorporating coping activities into your social time with them. These might include things such as exercising, eating healthy, meditation, and other activities outlined previously in this guide.

If they do accept that they are depressed, try finding out why they feel that way and see if you can do anything for them. Listening is key. Since individuals with low self-esteem tend to feel worse when told to "cheer up," avoid using positive enforcers when communicating *(Marigold)*. This is because positive enforcement makes a person's negative experiences feel unacknowledged. Let them have space to talk and express their feelings and needs. In response empathize with them: "I'm so sorry that sounds like it must be really hard," or "those words must have made you feel upset." Sometimes people need to first feel heard before they can become open to listening to advice or taking care of themselves. If individuals keep bringing up the same complaints though, a polite conversation about letting go of their woes and moving forward might be in order. Sometimes it is necessary to bluntly call a person out on their less desirable traits and reveal truths they are unaware of, but see where empathy leads first. For a more thorough guide on expressing empathy, see Marshall B. Rosenberg's book, *Nonviolent Communication: A Language of Compassion*.

Providing empathy may be enough to draw a person out of a depressed state, but otherwise you'll need to analyze where their depression stems from. This may be different from what they say they're depressed about. Consider their lifestyle habits such as diet, exercise, social life, and getting outdoors. In the past, I have rationalized my depression through scorning different aspects of my life, when in reality it was likely caused by a combination of not getting outside enough, being malnourished, and living in a stressful environment. I simply found it easier to blame things like my appearance for being depressed rather than the root causes. Once you have some ideas, ask if you can make some suggestions. Even if your friend doesn't follow your advice, at the very least the ideas will be there if they change their mind. You can also get them a gift or express gratitude for their presence. A book that provides life tools may be easier for them to digest than straight advice from a friend. In fact, true healing is likely not possible unless we empower ourselves to do so with our own mental energy. You can help provide the tools, but your friend must use them.

13.4 - If Someone You Care about Has Suicidal Ideations or Attempts Suicide

If you believe that someone close to you is considering killing themselves, there are things you can do to help prevent it.

While some people commit suicide with no warnings, those who are open about their feelings are in fact seeking help. Here are some actions you can take:

- Ask them directly if they are thinking of committing suicide, and have a conversation about it. If they want it, help connect them with professional mental support. A person depressed enough to commit suicide may not have the energy to seek help themselves.

- Express empathy for their feelings with techniques outlined by Nonviolent Communication (Section 10.4). Tell them that the feelings they are experiencing will pass with time.

- Call 1-800-273-8255 for someone to talk to through the National Suicide Hotline. They can offer confidential guidance, support, and help connect you with local resources.

- Even if your loved one asks for secrecy, and even if it is uncomfortable, tell people who are legally responsible for their well-being, such as their parents or a partner. A person with suicidal ideations needs support, not silence.

- Remember, there is always help and hope, and that every day is a new day with new possibilities,

- Do not allow a person to manipulate you into believing that you are the only reason why they are alive. Seek mental support yourself for help navigating the emotional difficulties of a friend's suicidal ideations or attempts.

- For a more thorough guide on preventing suicide, see <www.helpguide.org/mental/suicide_prevention.htm>.

13.5 - Talking to a Medical Professional

You might hesitate about approaching a stranger to discuss your emotional state, but it can be really helpful to see a medical professional to help you cope with depression and depressed feelings. At the very least they will give you new options to utilize as coping mechanisms. Only you can say when the time is right to see a doctor, therapist, herbalist, or other medical professional, but here are some ideas:

- You feel miserable all the time no matter what you do.
- You hurt yourself or have thoughts of hurting yourself or others.
- You have suicidal thoughts.
- You cannot handle taking care of yourself and become unhealthy.
- You have repetitive negative thoughts.
- You have anxiety that interferes with your ability to live a healthy life or the life you want to live.
- You realize you need help.
- Your depression interferes with basic social, professional, or interpersonal functioning on a day-to-day basis.

Just keep in mind that some doctors will only recommend taking pharmaceutical medicines while in fact there are many other options to choose from, or pair with, pharmaceutical treatment. Medication is not a replacement for good self-care practices!

14

Resources

I strongly suggest exploring other resources, especially for a more thorough explanation of the techniques outlined throughout this guide. Each perspective has its own strengths for giving you a better image of mental health and how to handle it or help others.

14.1 – Books

Nonviolent Communication: A Language of Compassion

In this book Marshall B. Rosenberg describes nonviolent communication (NVC), a very effective style of communication which relates all feelings and judgments to unmet needs. It covers much more than that though, including tools for practicing empathy, an analysis of hostile language commonly used in the United States, communicating with ourselves internally, how to express anger effectively, what it means not to judge others, and diffusing arguments. This book changed my life and I think it is essential in a world where very few have been taught how to communicate. It is well paired with video examples and local workshops. <www.cnvc.org>

Pronoia Is The Antidote for Paranoia

Rob Brezsny presents an inspiring case for how amazing each and every one of our lives are. Normally found in weekly newspapers with his horoscope, Free Will Astrology, Brezsny's book pieces together why we are lucky and should be overflowing with joy every moment, even in the midst of difficult circumstances. This book is not for everyone, but in combination with *Nonviolent Communication: A Language of Compassion,* it is what finally helped me get and stay out of a three year depression. It is especially suggested for people who are tired of really serious self-help books and want something off-the-wall silly.
<www.freewillastrology.com>

The Heart of the Buddha's Teaching

In this book, Thich Nhat Hanh presents the fundamental teachings of Buddhist practice. These teachings are not so much religious or spiritual ones as they are a step-by-step guide to controlling emotions, learning mindfulness, navigating through suffering, and finding happiness and love in life.

That Which You Are Seeking Is Causing You to Seek

In this short book Cheri Huber presents a compilation of Zen inspired teachings about how different thought patterns create suffering. All ideas are well explained and formatted in such a way that make them easy to digest. I personally don't agree with everything written, but overall it is a great book to read many times over.

Quiet

Susan Cain presents a thorough analysis of introverts and extroverts, detailing important factors that keep the different mindsets content and happy.

Communicating Across the Divides in Our Everyday Lives

Don Schneider's book, *Communicating Across The Divides In Our Everyday Lives,* is a "psychological field manual for constructive dialogue about social and environmental concerns and the progress of civilization" (Schneider). It talks about different character styles that people communicate through and how to create meaningful conversations with people who disagree with your world views.

Man's Search for Meaning

Viktor Frankl writes about what creates true meaning in one's life.

The Power of Habit

Charles Duhigg explores how habits are formed and deformed.

How to Train a Wild Elephant & Other Adventures in Mindfulness

A book about practicing mindfulness. It includes many exercises and practices.

14.2 – Online and Local Resources

The Five and Fourteen Mindfulness Trainings

The Fourteen Mindfulness Trainings are a shorthand version of core Buddhist concepts westernized for easier understanding by Thich Nhat Hanh. He has also compiled them into an even shorter series known as the *Five Mindfulness Trainings*. They are not dogma, but rather good reminders for sources of suffering in life. I enjoy reading one or the other at least once a month because there is always some new insight to discover with the words packed so full of meaning. Both the *Five* and the *Fourteen Mindfulness Trainings* can be formally taken as vows in Thich Nhat Hanh's tradition, though even then, they are not dogma, but rather ideologies to strive for. This type of commitment is a very powerful method of habit reformation, and many people use it to help work through their suffering. Find the *Five* and the *Fourteen Mindfluness Trainings* at <www.plumvillage.org>.

The Icarus Project

"We are a network of people living with and/or affected by experiences that are commonly diagnosed and labeled as psychiatric conditions. We believe these experiences are mad gifts needing cultivation and care, rather than diseases or disorders. By joining together as individuals and as a community, the intertwined threads of madness, creativity, and collaboration can inspire hope and transformation in an oppressive and damaged world. Participation in The Icarus Project helps us overcome alienation and tap into the true potential that lies between brilliance and madness." The Icarus Project website includes many free booklets covering various aspects of mental health.
<http://theicarusproject.net/>

Mind Freedom International

"In a spirit of mutual cooperation, MindFreedom leads a nonviolent revolution of freedom, equality, truth and human rights that unites people affected by the mental health system with movements for justice everywhere."

Ted Talks

Ted Talks provides hundreds of informational seminar videos on different subjects. Ten to twenty minutes in length, they are often uplifting or provide insights into the amazing mental and physical abilities humans have inherent access to.
<www.tedtalks.com>

Search Engines

When you come across a situation you've never encountered, or are unsure how to proceed with one, use a search engine. Someone has probably gone through the same thing as you and written a guide about it online. These often include advice on how to navigate a situation, what to do in the future, and steps to speed recovery. Search engines are also helpful in finding support groups, therapists, etc. in your area.

AllAboutDepression.com

"For more than 10 years providing accurate, current, and relevant information about clinical depression to the public."
<www.allaboutdepression.com>

Elephant Journal

The Elephant Journal has a great selection of short, thoughtful, and conscious articles that help illuminate how to navigate life. The articles vary in quality, but there are some gems everyday.

15
Conclusion

I hope you have found inspiration and hope in the many options provided in this guide. This started as a simple research project without much direction, but became much more than that in the nearly three years it took to get to this point. In fact, it was more an exploration of myself, and a personal log of what worked and what did not work as I battled with ups and downs through love and loss, family and friends, and my own brain conundrums. I must admit to ignoring my mental health more frequently than I would like to have, but I'm glad to have seen a project to completion, and to now understand so much more about what it takes to be content and happy. Each and every day there is a new challenge to face, but with the right tools, with the right communities, and with the right thinking, I know it is possible to feel happily fulfilled. I wish you good luck in your endeavors toward finding the place you want to be!

16
Bibliography

American Cancer Society, Inc. "Vitamin B Complex." *Cancer.org*. May 2010. Web. 24 Apr. 2012.

Amin, Zenab, Turhan Canli, and C. Neill Epperson. "Effect of Estrogen-Serotonin Interactions on Mood and Cognition." *Behavioral and Cognitive Neuroscience Reviews* 4.1 (Mar. 2005): 43-58. *Sage Publications. Behavioral and Cognitive Neuroscience.* Web. 9 Jan. 2015. DOI: 10.1177/1534582305277152

Arasteh, Kamyar. "A Beneficial Effect of Calcium Intake on Mood." *Journal of Orthomolecular Medicine* 9.4 (1994): 199-204. *The Center For The Improvement Of Human Functioning International.* Web. 10 May 2012.

Arnstein Mykletun, et al. "Association Between Magnesium Intake And Depression And Anxiety In Community-Dwelling Adults: The Hordaland Health Study." *The Australian And New Zealand Journal Of Psychiatry* 43.1 (2009): 45-52. *MEDLINE.* Web. 10 May 2012.

Bair, Asatar. "8 Basic Kinds of Meditation (And Why You Should Meditate On Your Heart)." *Institute for Applied Meditation.* 12 Jun. 2010. Web. 23 Oct. 2014.

Bao, Ai-Min, et al. "Diurnal rhythm of free estradiol during the menstrual cycle." European Journal of Endocrinology 148 (2003): 227-232. European Journal of Endocrinology. Web. 10 Jan. 2015.

Bashir N., et al. "The ironic impact of activists: Negative stereotypes reduce social change influence." *European Journal of Social Psychology* 43.7 (Dec. 2013): 614-626. *Wiley Online Library.* Web. 30 Jun. 2014. doi: 10.1002/ejsp.1983

Beck, Taylor. "Estrogen and female anxiety." *Harvard Gazette.* 9 Aug. 2012. Web. 9 Jan. 2014.

Benton, David. "Selenium Intake, Mood and Other Aspects of Psychological Functioning." *Nutritional Neuroscience* 5.6 (Jan 2001): 363-374(12). Web. 10 May 2012. doi: http://dx.doi.org/10.1080/1028415021000055925. Ingenta Connect. Web. 10 May 2012.

Bhatia, Subhash C., and Shashi K. Bhatia. "Diagnosis and Treatment of Premenstrual Dysphoric Disorder." *American Family Physician* 66.7 (1 Oct. 2002): 1239-1249. Web. 9 Nov. 2013.

BioMed Central. "Global depression statistics." *ScienceDaily,* 25 Jul. 2011. Web. 20 Feb. 2012.

Boelens, PA, RR Reeves, WH Replogle, and HG Koenig. "A Randomized Trial of the Effect of Prayer on Depression and Anxiety." *International Journal of Psychiatry in Medicine* 39.4 (2009): 377-392.

Brauser, Deborah. "Psychedelic Drugs May Reduce Symptoms of Depression, Anxiety, and OCD." *MedScape News Today.* 25 Aug 2010. Web. 25 Feb 2012.

"Breakfast." *Wiktionary. Wikimedia Project.* 27 Nov. 2014. Web. 11 Dec. 2014.

Brezsny, Rob. *Pronoia.* Berkeley: North Atlantic Books, 2009. Print.

Brown, Brene. "The power of vulnerability." Online video clip. *TED.* TEDxHouston. Filmed Jun. 2010. Web. 7 Aug. 2014.

B.S. Gupta and Uma Gupta. "Caffeine and Behavior." P. 21. 1999. *Google Books*. No Date. Web. 29 March 2012.

Busch, Sandi. "Wheat Bran Nutrition Information." *Livestrong*. 11 Mar. 2011. Web. 8 Aug. 2012.

Cajochen, Christian, et al. "Evidence that the Lunar Cycle Influences Human Sleep." *Current Biology* 23.15 (5 Aug. 2013): 1485-1488. *Cell Press*. Web. 8 Dec. 2014. doi: http://dx.doi.org/10.1016/j.cub.2013.06.029

C. Stough, et al. "Chronic MDMA (Ecstasy) Use, Cognition And Mood." *Psychopharmacology* 173.3/4 (2004): 434-439. *Academic Search Premier*. Web. 20 Feb. 2012.

Cain, Susan. *Quiet*. New York: Broadway Paperbacks, 2013. Print.

"Carbon Dioxide." *Wisconsin Department of Health Services*. 7 Aug. 2013. Web. 27 Aug 2013.

Carpenter, David, J. "St. John's Wort And S-Adenosyl Methionine As "Natural" Alternative To Conventional Antidepressants In The Era Of The Suicidality Boxed Warning: What Is The Evidence For Clinically Relevent Benefit?." *Alternative Medicine Review* 16.1 (2011): 17-39. *CINAHL with Full Text*. Web. 25 Mar. 2012.

Carrillo, J.A., and J. Benitez. "Clinically Significant Pharmacokinetic Interactions Between Dietary Caffeine And Medications." *Clinical Pharmacokinetics* 39.2 (2000): 127-153. *Academic Search Premier*. Web. 29 Mar. 2012.

Childs E, Hohoff, et al. "Association Between ADORA2A and DRD2 Polymorphisms and Caffeine-Induced Anxiety." *Neuropsychopharmacology* (2008) 33:2791-2800. *National Institute of Health Public Access*. Web. 29 March 2012.

Cloud, John. "Was Timothy Leary Right?" *Time Magazine*. 19 Apr 2007. Web. 25 Feb 2012.

Cohen, M, N Solowij, and V Carr. "Cannabis,

Cannabinoids And Schizophrenia: Integration Of The Evidence." *Australian & New Zealand Journal Of Psychiatry* 42.5 (2008): 357-368. *CINAHL with Full Text*. Web. 21 Feb. 2012.

Coulston, CM, M Perdices, and CC Tennant. "The Neuropsychology Of Cannabis And Other Substance Use In Schizophrenia: Review Of The Literature And Critical Evaluation Of Methodological Issues." *Australian & New Zealand Journal Of Psychiatry* 41.11 (2007): 869-884. *CINAHL with Full Text*. Web. 22 Feb. 2012.

Columbia University. "Q & A On Bright Light Therapy." No date. Web. 24 Feb 2012.

"Crocus sativus: Saffron Crocus." White Flower Farm. No Date. Web. 26 Mar 2012.

Crowther, Penny. "Vitamin D: Why We Need More Of The Sunshine Vitamin." *Positive Health* 167 (2010): 1. *Alt HealthWatch*. Web. 20 Feb. 2012.

Cuda, Gretchen. "Just Breathe: Body Has A Built-In Stress Reliever." *NPR Books*. 06 Dec. 2010. Web. 28 March 2014.

Cuddy, Amy. "You body language shapes who you are." Online video clip. *TED*. TED. Filmed Jun. 2012. Web. 7 Aug. 2014.

Darakhshan J. Haleem, et al. "Long-Term Consumption Of Sugar-Rich Diet Decreases The Effectiveness Of Somatodendritic Serotonin-1A Receptors." *Nutritional Neuroscience* 11.6 (2008): 277-282. *Academic Search Premier*. Web. 10 Apr. 2012.

Davison, K. Michelle. "The Determinants of Food Intake in Individuals with Mood Disorders." *University of Calgary. DSpace.* Jan. 2010. Web. 10 Apr. 2012.

Davison, Karen M., and Bonnie J. Kaplan. "Nutrient Intakes Are Correlated With Overall Psychiatric Functioning In Adults With Mood Disorders." *Canadian Journal Of Psychiatry* 57.2 (2012): 85-92. *Academic Search Premier*. Web. 10 May 2012.

Daw, Jennifer. "Is PMDD real?" *Monitor on Psychology* 33.9

(Oct. 2002): 58. *American Psychological Association*. Web. 9 Nov. 2013.

Deans, Emily, M.D. "Could Soda and Sugar Be Causing Your Depression?" *Psychology Today. Sussex Publishers, LLC.* 24 May 2011. Web. 8 Feb 2012.

Degenhardt, L, W Hall, and M Lynskey. "Exploring The Association Between Cannabis Use And Depression." *Addiction* 98.11 (2003): 1493-1504. *CINAHL with Full Text.* Web. 21 Feb. 2012.

Delude, Cathryn M. "Brain researchers explain why old habits die hard." *MIT News.* 19 Oct 2005. Web. 20 Jun 2013.

Diamond, Jed. "What Your Doctor Won't Tell You about Male Hormonal Cycles." *Goodtherapy.org.* 9 Oct. 2012. Web. 8 Jan. 2015.

"Dietary Supplement Fact Sheet: Vitamin D." *Office of Dietary Supplements. National Institutes of Health. USA.gov.* No date. Web. 15 Jul 2012.

Donovan, Patricia. "Afterbirth: Study Asks If We Could Derive Benefits from Ingesting Placenta. *University of Buffalo. News Center.* 27 Mar. 2012. Web. 8 Aug. 2012.

Dwyer, Anna, V., Dawn, L. Whitten, and Jason, A. Hawrelak. "Herbal Medicines, Other Than St. John's Wort, In The Treatment Of Depression: A Systematic Review." *Alternative Medicine Review* 16.1 (2011): 40-49. *CINAHL with Full Text.* Web. 22 Feb. 2012.

"Dysthymia." *Mayo Clinic.* 20 Dec. 2012. Web. 8 Nov. 2013.

E Singh, et al. "Diversified potentials of *Ocimum sanctum* Linn (Tulsi): An exhaustive survey." *Journal of Natural Product and Plant Resource.* 2012, 2 (1): 39-48. *Scholars Research Library.* Web. 19 Aug. 2013.

Edberg, Henrik. "How to Create an Abundance Mentality."

The Positivity Blog. 30 Jan. 2008. Web. 16 Nov. 2012.

European College of Neuropsychopharmacology. "Birth season affects your mood in later life, new research suggests." ScienceDaily. ScienceDaily, 18 October 2014. Web. 7 Jan. 2015.

Evans, Dr. Mike. "23 and 1/2 Hours" Online Video. YouTube. 2 Dec 2011. Web. 20 Feb 2012.

Field T, Diego M, and Hernandez-Reif M. "Moderate pressure is essential for massage therapy effects." *International Journal of Neuroscience* 120.5 (May 2010): 381-385. *US National Library of Medicine*. Web. 23 Sep. 2013. doi: 10.3109/00207450903579475

Field, Tiffany M. "Massage therapy effects." *American Psychologist* 53.12 (Dec. 1998): 1270-1281. Web. 10 Sep. 2013. doi: 10.1037/0003-066X.53.12.1270

Fournier J, et al. "Antidepressant Drug Effects and Depression Severity." *The Journal of the American Medical Association* 303.1 (2010): 47-53. Web. 25 Mar. 2012. doi: 10.1001/jama.2009.1943

G. Singh, et al. "Biological activities of Withania somnifera." *Annuals of Biological Research* 1.3 (2010): 56-63. *Scholars Research Library*. Web. 15 Oct. 2013.

Gail C. Farmer, et al. "Alcohol Use And Depression Symptoms Among Employed Men And Women." *American Journal Of Public Health* 77.6 (1987): 704-707. *Academic Search Premier*. Web. 20 Feb. 2012.

Gardiner, P, and KJ Kemper. "Natural" Remedies For Depression: Are They Safe? Do They Work?" *Contemporary Pediatrics* 23.9 (2006): 58. *CINAHL with Full Text*. Web. 5 Apr. 2012.

Gregoire, Carolyn. "The Surprising Link Between Gut Bacteria And Anxiety." Huffington Post. Science. 4 Jan. 2015. Web. 9 Jan. 2015.

"Griffonia simplicifolia." *Siris Impex.* No Date. Web. 24 Apr. 2012.

Grish, Kristina. "Dealing with PMS: The Benefits of Being Premenstural." *Women's Health.* 18 Nov. 2005. Web. 12 Jan. 2015.

Grohol, John M.. "Is Mindfulness-based Cognitive Therapy Effectiive?" *PsychCentral.* Web. 22 Feb. 2012.

Gross, Terry. "Bacterial Bonanza: Microbes Keep Us Alive." *NPR Fresh Air from WHYY.* 15 Sept. 2010. Web. 26 Jun. 2013.

Gross, Terry. "Habits: How They Form And How To Break Them." *NPR Fresh Air from WHYY.* 5 Mar. 2012. Web. 24 Jun. 2013.

Harrison, Lewis. *Healing Depression Naturally.* U.S.A.: Kensington, 2004. P. 63. Print.

Head, KA, and GS Kelly. "Nutrients And Botanicals For Treatment Of Stress: Adrenal Fatigue, Neurotransmitter Imbalance, Anxiety, And Restless Sleep." *Alternative Medicine Review* 14.2 (2009): 114-140. *CINAHL with Full Text.* Web. 22 Feb. 2012.

Hirschfeld RM. "History and evolution of the monoamine hypothesis of depression." *Journal of Clinical Psychiatry* 61 Suppl 6 (2000): 4-6. *US National Library of Medicine. PubMed.* Web. 11 May 2012.

Holick, Michael F. "Sunlight and vitamin D for bone health and prevention of autoimmune diseases, cancers, and cardiovascular disease." *The American Journal of Clinical Nutrition* 80.6 (Dec. 2004): 1678S-1688S. Web. 7 Sep. 2013.

"How Much Sleep Do We Really Need?" *National Sleep Foundation.* No Date. Web. 26 Mar 2012.

Hughes, Edward. "Art Therapy As A Healing Tool For Sub-Fertile Women." *Journal Of Medical Humanities* 31.1 (2010): 27-36. *Academic Search Premier.* Web. 2 Mar. 2012.

J Sanmukhani, et al. "Efficacy and Safety of Curcumin in Major Depressive Disorder: A Randomized Controlled Trial."

National Center for Biotechnology Information. U.S. National Library of Medicine. 6 Jul. 2013. Web. 17 Aug. 2013. doi: 10.1002/ptr.5025

Jackson, Justine. "Animal-Assisted Therapy: The Human-Animal Bond In Relation To Human Health and Wellness." *Winona State University*. P. 7-8. Spring 2012. Web. 6 Dec 2014.

"Jessica Green: Are we filtering the wrong microbes?" Jessica Green. *Ted Talks*. Aug. 2011. Web. 17 Apr. 2012.

Johnson JM, Nachtigall Lb, and Stern TA. "The effect of testosterone levels on mood in men: a review." *Psychosomatics* 54.6 (2013 Nov-Dec): 509-14. *US National Library of Medicine. PubMed*. Web. 9 Jan. 2015. doi: 10.1016/j.psym.2013.06.018.

Judith Paice, et al. "Art Therapy For Relief Of Symptoms Associated With HIV/AIDS." *AIDS Care* 21.1 (2009): 64-69. *MEDLINE*. Web. 2 Mar. 2012.

Kahneman, Daniel and Angus Deaton. "High income improves evaluation of life but not emotional well-being." *Proceedings of the National Academy of Sciences of the United States of America* 107.38 (21 Sep. 2010): 16489-16493. Web. 19 Sep. 2014.

Kemper, Kathi, and Suzanne Danhauer. "Music as Therapy." *Southern Medical Journal* 98.3 (2005): 282-288. *US National Library of Medicine. PubMed*. Web. 8 Dec. 2014.

Kenneth O. Carter, Michelle Olshan-Perlmutter, H. James Norton, and Michael O. Smith. "NADA Acupuncture Prospective Trial in Patients with Substance Use Disorders and Seven Common Health Symptoms." *Medical Acupuncture* 23.3 (Sep. 2011): 131-135. Web. 23 Sep. 2013. doi:10.1089/acu.2010.0784

Kim, Pilyoung, et al. "Effects of childhood poverty and chronic stress on emotion regulatory brain function in adulthood." *Proceedings of the National Academy of Sciences of the United States of America* (21 Oct. 2013). Web. 25 Oct. 2013. doi:

10.1073/pnas.1308240110

Kirsch I, Deacon BJ, Huedo-Medina TB, Scoboria A, Moore TJ, et al. (2008) Initial Severity and Antidepressant Benefits: A Meta-Analysis of Data Submitted to the Food and Drug Administration. *PLoS Med* 5.2 (28 Feb 2008): e45. Web. 4 Apr. 2012. doi:10.1371/journal.pmed.0050045

Klein, Sarah. "Inflammatory Foods: 9 Of The Worst Picks For Inflammation." *The Huffington Post*. 21 Mar. 2013. Web. 10 Jan. 2015.

Kresser, Chris. "Is Depression a Disease-or a Symptom of Inflammation?" *Chris Kresser.* Nov. 2014. Web. 11 Jan. 2015.

Krishnan, Vaishnav and Nestler, Eric. "Linking Molecules to Mood: New Insight Into the Biology of Depression." *American Journal of Psychiatry* 167.11 (Nov. 2010): 1305-1320. Web. 25 Apr. 2012. doi: 10.1176/appi.ajp.2009.10030434

Kross E, Verduyn P, Demiralp E, Park J, Lee DS, et al. "Facebook Use Predicts Declines in Subjective Well-Being in Young Adults." *PLoS ONE* 8.8: e69841. 14 Aug. 2013. Web. 29 Aug. 2013. doi:10.1371/journal.pone.0069841

Kwak, Hae-Soo, ed. *Nano- and Microencapsulation for Foods*. p. 227. West Sussex, UK: John Wiley & Sons, Ltd 2014. *Google Book Search*. Web. 8 Dec. 2014.

Laura A. G. Armas, et al. "Vitamin D2 Is Much Less Effective than Vitamin D3 in Humans." *The Journal of Clinical Endocrinology & Metabolism* 89.11 (Nov. 2004): 5387-5391. Web. 22 Jul. 2012. doi: 10.1210/jc.2004-0360

Law, Bridget M. "Probing the depression-rumination cycle." *American Psychological Association*. 36.10 (Nov. 2005): 38. Web. 15 Sep. 2013.

Layton, Julia. "Is it true that if you do anything for three weeks it will become a habit?" *howstuffworks*. No date. Web. 20 Jun. 2013.

Lazar, Sara. "The Science of Mindfulness and Meditation." University of Oregon, Willamette Hall, Room 110. Eugene, OR. 1 Nov. 2013. Symposium.

Levenson, CW. "Zinc: The New Antidepressant?" *Nutrition Reviews* 64.1 (2006): 39-42. *CINAHL with Full Text*. Web. 4 May 2012.

Levinson, F. Douglas and Walter E. Nichols. "Major Depression and Genetics." *Stanford School of Medicine. Stanford University*. No date. Web. 28 Oct. 2013.

Lienhard H, John. "No. 883: Smiles That Make You Happy." *Engines of Our Ingenuity. University of Houston*. No Date. Web. Apr 14, 2012.

Logan, Alan C. "Omega-3 fatty acids and major depression: A primer for the mental health professional." *Lipids in Health and Disease*. 3: 25 (Nov. 2004). *US National Library of Medicine*. *PubMed*. Web. 2 Sep. 2012. doi: 10.1186/1476-511X-3-25

Lokuge S, Frey BN, Foster JA, Soares CN, Steiner M. "Depression in women: windows of vulnerability and new insights into the link between estrogen and serotonin." *Journal of Clinical Psychiatry* 72.11 (Nov. 2011): e1563-9. Web. 10 Jan. 2015.

Macy, Joanna. "The Work That Reconnects." *Work That Reconnects Network*. n.d. Web. 20 Sep. 2014.

M Brown, et al. "Dampness And Mold In The Home And Depression: An Examination Of Mold-Related Illness And Perceived Control Of One's Home As Possible Depression Pathways." *American Journal Of Public Health* 97.10 (2007): 1893-1899. *CINAHL with Full Text*. Web. 22 Feb. 2012.

Marano, Daniel A. "Soil Salvation." *Psychology Today* 41.5 (2008): 57-58. *Academic Search Premier. EBSCO*. Web. 6 Nov. 2009.

Marigold DC, Cavallo JV, Homes JG, Wood JV. "You can't always give what you want: The challenge of providing social support to low self-esteem individuals." *Journal of Personality and Social Psychology.* 107.1. (Jul, 2014): 56-80. doi: 10.1037/a0036554. *US National Library of Medicine. National Center for Biotechnology Information.* Web. 29 Jun. 2014.

McGregor, Ian and Brian R. Little. "Personal Projects, Happiness, and Meaning: On Doing Well and Being Yourself." *Journal of Personality and Social Psychology* 74.2 (1998): 494-512. *US National Library of Medicine. National Center for Biotechnology Information.* Web. 14 Oct. 2013.

"Meditation In Psychotherapy. An Ancient Spiritual Practice Is Finding New Uses In The Treatment Of Mental Illness." *The Harvard Mental Health Letter / From Harvard Medical School* 21.10 (2005): 1-4. *MEDLINE.* Web. 21 Feb. 2012.

MedlinePlus. "Depression." *U.S. National Library of Medicine. National Institutes of Health.* 25 Mar. 2012. Web. 8 Jul. 2013.

Miller, A. K. H.; Alston, Corsellis. "VARIATION WITH AGE IN THE VOLUMES OF GREY AND WHITE MATTER IN THE CEREBRAL HEMISPHERES OF MAN: MEASUREMENTS WITH AN IMAGE ANALYSER." *Neuropathology and Applied Neurobiology* 6.2: 119–132. 28 Jun. 2013. doi:10.1111/j.1365-2990.1980.tb00283.x. PMID 7374914

Nelson, Craig J.. "The Evolving Story of Folate in Depression and the Therapeutic Potential of L-Methylfolate." *American Journal of Psychiatry* 169 (1 Dec. 2012): 1223-1225. *Psychology Online.* Web. 18 Jul. 2014. doi:10.1176/appi.ajp.2012.12091207

Newitz, Annalee. "Eat a Lunch That Keeps You Productive All Afternoon." *Life Hacker.* 24 Aug. 2007. Web. 24 Feb. 2012.

Nonviolent Communication Training Course. Dir. Marshall B. Rosenberg. The Center For Nonviolent Communication, 2010. Audio CD. CD #3.

Paula Goolkasian, et al. "Effects Of Brief And Sham Mindfulness Meditation On Mood And Cardiovascular Variables." *Journal Of Alternative & Complementary Medicine* 16.8 (2010): 867-873. *CINAHL with Full Text*. Web. 22 Feb. 2012.

Pearlstein, Teri and Meir Steiner. "Premenstrual dysphoric disorder: burden of illness and treatment update." *Journal of Psychiatry Neuroscience* 33.4 (Jul. 2008): 291-301. *National Center for Biotechnology Information*. Web. 8 Nov. 2013.

"Phosphorus." University of Maryland Medical Center. 17 Jun. 2012. Web. 12 May 2012.

"Poor Diet Link To Depression And Anxiety." *Australian Nursing Journal* 19.3 (2011): 20. *CINAHL with Full Text*. Web. 8 Feb. 2012.

"Principles, The." *Center For Sustainable Change*. n.d. Web. Sep. 20, 2014.

procon.org. "Is medical marijuana an effective treatment for depression, bipolar disorders, anxiety, and similar mood disorders?" May 2005. Web. 8 Feb. 2012.

Rezaei, Ali, Eilyard Issabeagloo, and Javadsadigi Kordlar. "Study of Sedative, Preanaestheticand Anti-anxiety Effects of Herbal Extract of Motherwort (Leonuruscardiac) in Comparison with Diazepam in rat." *Bulletin of Environment, Pharmacology and Life Sciences* 3.2 (Jan. 2014): 67-71. *Academy for Environment and Life Sciences, India*. Web. 8 Aug. 2014.

Richard, Michael. "Best Air-Filtering House Plants According to NASA!" *Mother Nature* Network. 9 Feb 2009. Web. 21 Feb 2012.

Rosenberg, Marshall. *Nonviolent Communication: A Language of Compassion*. Encinitas: Puddle Dancer Press, 2002. Print.

Ross J. Baldessarini, et al. "Coffee And Cigarette Use: Association With Suicidal Acts In 352 Sardinian Bipolar Disorder

Patients." *Bipolar Disorders* 11.5 (2009): 494-503. *Academic Search Premier*. Web. 20 Feb. 2012.

Ruiz-Belda, María-Angeles, José-Miguel Fernández-Dols, and Kim Barchard. "Spontaneous Facial Expressions Of Happy Bowlers And Soccer Fans." *Cognition & Emotion* 17.2 (2003): 315. *Academic Search Premier*. Web. 15 Apr. 2012.

Russell Geen et al. "The Facilitation of Aggression by Aggression: Evidence against the Catharsis Hypothesis." *Journal of Personality and Social Psychology* 31.4 (Apr. 1975): 721-26. *US National Library of Medicine. National Institutes of Health*. Web. 13 Oct. 2013.

S. Meir, et al. "Expert Guidelines for the Treatment of Severe PMS, PMDD, and Comorbidities: The Role of SSRIs." *Journal of Women's Health* 15.1 (17 Jan. 2006): 57-69. Web. 8 Nov. 2013. doi:10.1089/jwh.2006.15.57

S. Korkmaz, et al. "Effects Of Green Buildings On Employee Health And Productivity." *American Journal Of Public Health* 100.9 (2010): 1665-1668. *CINAHL with Full Text*. Web. 22 Feb. 2012.

S. Steinberg, et al. "A Placebo-Controlled Study of the Effects of L-Tryptophan in Patients with Premenstrual Dysphoria." *Tryptophan, Serotonin, and Melatonin Advances in Experimental Medicine and Biology* 467 (1999): 85-88. *Springer Link*. Web. 8 Nov. 2013.

Scheel, KR, and JS Westefeld. "Heavy Metal Music and Adolescent Suicidality: An Empirical Investigation." *Adolescence* 34.134 (1999): 253-273.

Schimelpfening, Nancy. "What Are Cognitive Distortions?" *About Health*. Depression Coping Skills. 19 Dec. 2014. Web. 22 Dec. 2014.

Schneider, Don. *Communicating Across The Divides In Our Everyday Lives*. Elkdream Media. Dec. 2009. Front cover. Print.

Seligman ME, et al. "Positive psychology progress: empirical validation of interventions." *American Psychological Association* 60.5 (Jul.-Aug. 2005): 410-21. *US National Library of Medicine.* Web. 29 Oct. 2013.

Shaw, Kelly, Jane Turner, and Christopher Del Mar. "Are Tryptophan And 5-Hydroxytryptophan Effective Treatments For Depression? A Meta-Analysis*." *Australian & New Zealand Journal Of Psychiatry* 36.4 (2002): 488-491. *Academic Search Premier.* Web. 20 Feb. 2012.

Simopoulos AP. "The importance of the ratio of omega-6/omega-3 essential fatty acids." Biomedicine and Pharmacotherapy 56(8) (Oct 2002): 365-79. The Center for Genetics, Nutrition and Health. PubMed. Web. 12 May 2012.

Siple, Molly. "Anti-Inflammatory Diet." Natural Health Mag. The American Media. No Date. Web. 10 Jan. 2015.

Smith, Andrew P. "Caffeine, Cognitive Failures And Health In A Non-Working Community Sample." *Human Psychopharmacology: Clinical & Experimental* 24.1 (2009): 29-34. *Academic Search Premier. Web.* 20 Feb. 2012.

Smith, Andrew P. and Amanda Wilds. "Effects of cereal bars for breakfast and mid-morning snacks on mood and memory." *International Journal of Food Sciences and Nutrition* 60.s4 (2009): 63-69. Web. 29 Dec. 2013. doi:10.1080/09637480802438305)

Smith, Caroline A, Phillipa PJ Hay, Hugh Macpherson. "Acupuncture for depression." *John Wiley & Sons, Ltd.* (Jan 2010). The Cochrane Library. Web. 23 Sep. 2013. doi: 10.1002/14651858.CD004046.pub3

Smith, Emily Esfahani. "There's More to Life Than Being Happy." *The Atlantic.* 2013 Jan 9. Web. 27 Feb. 2013.

Smith, Melinda, et al. "How to Sleep Better." *HelpGuide.Org.* Dec. 2011. Web. 25 Feb. 2012.

Sperm Bank, Inc. "8 Benefits of Male Masturbation." No

date. Web. 25 Feb. 2012.

Szabadi, E. "St. John's Wort And Its Active Principles In Depression And Anxiety." *British Journal Of Clinical Pharmacology* 62.3 (2006): 377-378. *Academic Search Premier.* Web. 20 Feb. 2012.

Szalavitz, Maia. "Ecstasy as Therapy: Have Some of its Negative Effects Been Overblown?" *Time Healthland.* 18 Feb. 2011. Web. 25 Feb. 2012.

Todd, Nivin. "Estrogen and Women's Emotions." *WebMD.* 31 May 2012. Web. 9 Jan. 2015.

Trapani, Gina. "Top 10 Ways to Sleep Smarter and Better." *Life Hacker.* 10 Oct. 2007. Web. 24 Feb. 2012.

U Koch, et al. "Depression, Anxiety, Post-Traumatic Stress Disorder And Health-Related Quality Of Life And Its Association With Social Support In Ambulatory Prostate Cancer Patients." *European Journal Of Cancer Care* 19.6 (2010): 736-745. *CINAHL with Full Text.* Web. 22 Feb. 2012.

Vann, Madeline. "10 Healthy Ways to Manage PMS." *Everyday Health.* 12 Mar. 2012. Web. 12 Jan. 2015.

Villarreal, Christina. "Antidepressant medications: effective treatment for depression or pharmaceutical industry scam?" *examiner.com.* 26 Apr. 2010. Web. 25 Feb. 2012.

VITEX AGNUS - CASTUS. *WebMD.* N.D. Web. 8 Nov. 2013.

Weil, Andrew, M.D. "Q & A Library: Turmeric for Depression?" *Dr. Weil.* 26 Aug. 2013. Web. 17 Aug. 2013.

World's Healthiest Foods, The. "calcium." No date. Web. 10 May 2012.

World's Healthiest Foods, The. "folate." No date. Web. 20 Feb 2012.

World's Healthiest Foods, The. "iron." No date. Web. 12 May 2012.

World's Healthiest Foods, The. "magnesium." No date.

Web. 10 May 2012.

World's Healthiest Foods, The. "omega-3 fatty acids." No date. Web. 20 Feb 2012.

World's Healthiest Foods, The. "potassium." No date. Web. 12 May 2012.

World's Healthiest Foods, The. "selenium." No date. Web. 10 May 2012.

World's Healthiest Foods, The. "vitamin B12." No date. Web. 20 Feb 2012.

World's Healthiest Foods, The. "vitamin C." No date. Web. 10 May 2012.

World's Healthiest Foods, The. "zinc." No date. Web. 10 May 2012.

Williamson, C. "Dietary Factors And Depression In Older People." *British Journal Of Community Nursing* 14.10 (2009): 422. *CINAHL with Full Text*. Web. 8 Feb. 2012.

Wyatt, Katrina M., et al. "Efficacy of vitamin B-6 in the treatment of premenstrual syndrome: systematic review." *BMJ* 318.7195 (1999): 1375-1381. *National Center for Biotechnology Information*. Web. 8 Nov. 2013.

Young, Simon, N. "Bright Light For Nonseasonal Depression?" *Journal Of Psychiatry & Neuroscience* 36.5 (2011): E37-8. *CINAHL with Full Text*. Web. 23 Feb. 2012.

Zhang, Michelle, Line Robitaille, Shaun Eintracht, and L. John Hoffer. "Vitamin C Provision Improves Mood in Acutely Hospitalized Patients." *Nutrition* 27.5 (May 2011): 530-533. *US National Library of Medicine*. Web. 8 Dec. 2014. doi: 10.1016/j.nut.2010.05.016

Zhang-Jin Zhang, et al. "The effectiveness and safety of acupuncture therapy in depressive disorders: Systematic review and meta-analysis." *Journal of Affective Disorders* 124.1 (Jul. 2010): 9-21. Web. 23 Sep. 2013. doi: 10.1016/j.jad.2009.07.005)

My Mind

Adapted from the Icarus Project 'Mad Map.'

My Triggers

Things That Make Me Feel Better

People I Can Call

About the Author

Sage Liskey is an author, public speaker, peer counselor, community organizer, farmer, and artist based in the Pacific Northwest. Born and raised in Oregon, he now writes and leads workshops about community, sustainability and mental health. Visit <www.sageliskey.com> for upcoming events, informational booklets, and articles on personal growth and creating a better future.